The
Hostile
Sky

The Hostile Sky

A Hellcat Flier in World War II

James W. Vernon

Naval Institute Press
Annapolis, Maryland

Naval Institute Press
291 Wood Road
Annapolis, MD 21402

Library of Congress Cataloging-in-Publication Data
Vernon, James W., 1922–

  The hostile sky : a hellcat flier in World War II / James W. Vernon
A.

    p. cm.

  ISBN 1-55750-865-8 (alk. paper)

  1. Vernon, James W., 1922– 2. World War, 1939–1945—Personal narratives, American. 3. Fighter pilots—United States—Biography. 4. Hellcat (Fighter planes) 5. World War, 1939–1945—Campaigns—Pacific Ocean. I. Title.

  D811 .V363 2002

  940.54'4973'092—dc21

                                                          2002005546

Printed in the United States of America on acid-free paper ∞
10 09 08 07 06 05 04 03   9 8 7 6 5 4 3 2
First printing

To my wife, Doris Marshall Vernon

Contents

Preface   ix

1   Civilian Pilot Training   1

2   Flying Endlessly in Piper Cubs   12

3   Preflight School   16

4   On the Brink of Washing Out   29

5   Flying Those Turkey Vultee Vibrators   46

6   The End of a Long Beginning   52

7   Dive-Bombing at Cecil Field   66

8   Carrier Qualification on Lake Michigan   77

9   Joining Air Group 87   88

10   Routine Training Flights   100

11   Shakedown Cruise aboard the USS *Randolph*   110

12   Voyage to Hawaii   123

13   Night Field Carrier Landing Practice   130

14   Into Combat aboard the USS *Ticonderoga*   139

15   North to Japan with Task Group 38.3   152

16   We Regret to Inform You   157

17   Typhoon Season   169

18   A Waste of Men in a War Already Won   176

19   An Uncertain Future   186

20   On Leave after the War   193

21   Leaving the Peacetime Navy   197

     Index   203

Preface

We were the generation that went off to war, leaving behind worried and fearful parents, siblings, wives, sweethearts, and friends. As the war continued, worry and fear, with increasing frequency, changed to grief. We were forced to maturity by military discipline and responsibilities. We could not linger in adolescence, gradually preparing ourselves for life in a peaceful society. I was thrown together with many young men of about my age. Together we learned about flying and fighting an air war, and ultimately we were shipped halfway around the world to meet the enemy. Never before had America extended its reach on such an immense scale. The experience bound us together as a unique generation.

This story is about my effort to do what was expected of me and my reactions to military life during wartime—both the routine and the exceptional. I did nothing heroic, but I did what was required and had the luck to survive. I have attempted to tell my story in the voice of a young man, with the accuracy that memory allows. In places I have changed names to preserve the privacy of flying mates.

Anecdotes from this book have been printed in the U.S. Naval Institute's *Proceedings*. I thank them for permitting me to include them here. I gratefully acknowledge the criticisms and help from members of the Ventura County Writers Club, without which I would never have completed this book. My special thanks go to Claire Robey for her in-depth criticism and encouragement.

The
Hostile
Sky

I

Civilian Pilot Training

In early May 1945 the aircraft carrier USS *Ticonderoga* (CV14), the Big T, stood out to sea off Pearl Harbor and shaped a course to the war zone in the western Pacific. I was aboard as a fighter pilot in Air Group 87. After a short stop at Ulithi atoll in the western Caroline Islands, to join Task Force 38.4, we transited to Okinawa, where many of us first tasted combat. When Okinawa had been secured we moved offshore from the Japanese home islands, where we remained, making frequent strikes against airfields and anything that moved. After the atomic bombs were dropped and the surrender signed, we entered Tokyo Bay. Nothing in the two years of training had prepared me for the realities of war, the terror of brushes with disaster, the fatigue and boredom of flying over the endless ocean, and the deaths of flying mates.

Back in the spring and summer of 1942 the course of the war in the Pacific had shifted in our favor when our carrier task forces smashed the Japanese fleet at Midway; the heroes had been naval aviators in a war at sea in which aircraft carriers and their planes had replaced battleships as the main striking force. The Philippines, Singapore, Hong Kong, and the Netherlands East Indies had fallen to the Japanese, but our side was holding its own in New Guinea and winning the battle for Guadalcanal in the Solomon Islands.

At my age, nineteen, military service had been inevitable. I felt no impatience that it might all be over before I got into action. "Just take things as they come," I told myself, "and cover your backside." I had just completed two years of engineering at the Montana School of Mines, and I wanted a break from school, to do something different and stimulating. Military flying intrigued me. Although before the war I had had only a distant interest in flying, I decided that, since I had to enter the service, I should get involved in the rapidly evolving field of naval aviation.

Aviators, it seemed to me, had attained a status like locomotive engineers, stagecoach drivers, steamboat pilots, and ships' captains before them. They had captured the public's admiration because they had the power to push to the ends of the land and sea. A locomotive engineer in his high-crowned, striped cap leaning from his lofty window while controlling the raw power of whirling wheels and thrashing driveshafts with one hand, had awed me when I was a child. But now the roar of engines, the flash of propellers and silver wings overhead captured my imagination, as the aviator, unseen but potent, swiftly soared above and beyond the horizon. I sometimes wondered whether I dared to aspire to join their exclusive cult and whether they would let me in. But deep down I knew they were mere men—not much different from me. I was stimulated by the challenge and attracted to the drama of war in the air.

My decision to enter pilot training was mainly cerebral, colored by escapism, a sense of adventure, and yes, patriotism. I had never been in an airplane or even touched one on the ground. In the '30s I had visited a small airport in my hometown of Fargo, North Dakota, and seen a Ford Trimotor with its peculiar corrugated exterior, and I had walked in the shadow of its wings. I'd seen planes in flight, like the Douglas DC-2, which had a flight schedule through Fargo. I remember being with a group of boys on a country road near Fargo when one those planes flew over. "Give me a ride!" we screamed, like desperate castaways.

I hadn't read aviation fiction and I'm certain I never saw *Dawn Patrol* or any other movies about air combat in France during World War I. Model airplanes held no interest for me. During high school I had not considered joining the aeronautical program the school offered. Although I had become keenly interested in the air war being fought over Western Europe, it hadn't seemed relevant to me personally until Pearl Harbor.

In the summer of 1942 I enlisted in the Naval Aviation Cadet program and discovered that within the past few months the academic requirement for the program had been lowered from two years of college to high school graduation. That meant many of my fellow cadets would be fresh out of high school and a year or two younger than I. The full significance of this change wouldn't strike me until I went on active duty.

The Navy, having signed me up, then sent me home to Mother's dreary walk-up third floor apartment near Golden Gate Park in San Francisco to await orders. Mother, in her early fifties, was just under five feet, with a well-proportioned figure, large blue-green eyes, regular features, and graying hair. What didn't show was the tenacious will that had enabled her to raise four children while in conflict with a strong-willed, intelligent husband, and then support herself after their separation.

Her apartment house sat in a row of common-wall buildings adjacent to the sidewalk, with an open space at the rear separating it from the back of apartment houses facing the next street. A clothesline running through pulleys stretched from a window in her living room across an open space to the rear wall of those apartments. Mother's apartment had two bedrooms, a living room, kitchen, and bath. Furniture, tacky but adequate, reflected her small salary from the marine supply house where she worked. She fixed a bed for me in a barren bedroom with a streaky window looking into a bleak light shaft, and I settled in with her and her yellow tomcat. Mother seemed pleased that I wouldn't be shipped out immediately.

When my orders arrived, they directed me to report for civilian pilot training (CPT) at Lassen Junior College in Susanville, California, a hundred miles northwest of Reno. That disappointed me because I thought I would be sent to preflight school first. Since my old Chevy still ran reliably, I drove to Susanville, across the Central Valley, over the Sierra, and north along its eastern slope. Susanville sat in an irrigated farming area in a broad, semi-arid valley surrounded by sparsely forested and sagebrush-covered mountains. Single-storied, plate glass–faced businesses looked out onto the main street. Residences were mainly wooden, some two-storied. Cottonwood and elm trees, now denuded by early autumn frosts, lined the streets. The junior college consisted of an old, two-story, gray masonry building, which had once been the high school. I was to begin my naval aviation career in a remote farming town not too different from others I had known in the West. When I checked in, I was assigned a bunk in the improvised military barracks: a separate, spacious, one-room frame building with a high ceiling and wide door. I guessed it had once been a warehouse. On the main floor, bunks were arranged in rows, and a community lavatory occupied one corner. It turned out to be more comfortable than bunkhouses I had slept in at several of Dad's mining camps.

I found my bunk hung along the wall of a six-foot-wide mezzanine and looked around. Sprawled on nearby bunks were a couple of cadets; one, a powerfully built man, stood up and offered his hand and a salty "Welcome aboard. I'm Emmitt, just came in from Oakland. That's Bud over there. He's from Richmond. Where're you from?" Bud stood up smiling shyly and shook my hand; a shorty like me, he moved like an athlete, on the balls of his feet. "Don't listen to that guy," Bud said. "He went on like that on the bus all the way up to this cow town, except when he sketched anyone who'd sit still." We sat on a bunk and got acquainted. Bud, tough as the port city of Richmond, boxed as a golden glover, and Emmitt had played high school football in the Bay Area. We all spoke jockese.

"What do you say we check out the town?" Emmitt said. We walked the length of Main Street, picked out a bar, had a couple of drinks, told each other a few lies, and then wandered back to the barracks in the dark. Sleep came slowly that first night. My mind kept drifting to the future. Could I adapt to flying? And to the past, to the day my father and I had parted in San Francisco.

In my mind's eye I could still see Dad staring straight ahead, silently chewing a cigar, as I drove through hilly San Francisco and down Market Street to the Ferry Building, where he would catch a ferry to carry him across the bay to a train that would take him back to Montana. He cautiously broke his silence. "Jimmy, your mother doesn't care for me any more. We've been separated too long. It doesn't look like we'll get back together." He rolled down the window and tossed out his cigar butt. "I wish I hadn't come to visit." I had sensed his visit with her had not gone well, but it surprised me that he would talk about it. It saddened me to have my fears confirmed—that their marriage was nearing an end.

At the Ferry Building we stood silently on the curb as streetcars rattled past. His short compact body seemed to sag as the ferry's whistle moaned. We turned toward each other, made eye contact, shook hands, and hugged briefly. He paused, glancing pensively at the people boarding the ferry. Stealthily wiping his eye and then his glasses, he looked at me again and whispered, "Please be careful, Jimmy. Flying in the Navy will be dangerous."

I looked into his wet eyes—the first time I had seen him teary-eyed since our old dog had died from falling down a mineshaft—firmed my lips, and nodded. He swallowed hard, took a deep breath, squeezed my arm as though to assure me and himself that my entering the Navy was right, turned away, and picked up his suitcase. Squaring his shoulders and straightening his fedora, he strode away, head high, confident and defiant. The crowd swallowed him. My imminent entry into the Navy was as close as he would come to war. He had missed World War I because he was overage and had a wife and two children.

I felt sorry for him, a strong and lonely man, and to me, a tragic figure. I wished I could catch him and tell him everything was OK with Mother again, but I couldn't. He had become a loner, single-mindedly pursuing mining, the occupation he loved, but it had cost him his marriage and family life. Now I, too, had passed beyond his experience, into a world he could never know.

Fifty men trained at Susanville, a mixture of naval aviation cadets, still in civvies, training to be pilots, and Army Air Forces enlisted men in uniform, learning to be glider pilots. We cadets came mainly from the Bay Area and towns in the Central Valley: Madera, Sacramento, Stockton, Oildale, and Buttonwillow. We were strangers thrown together in an unfamiliar place, many away from home for the first time.

In ground school I discovered that the courses, aimed at the level of high school graduates, provided a review of mathematics and physics to cope with navigation and aerology. I also discovered that only I had studied these subjects at the college level. When the class caught on that I already knew a lot about these subjects, Bud, Emmitt, and others began to ask me for help with the daily assignments. That flattered me, as I had struggled to stay in the middle third of the class at the School of Mines. I realized then that, at the Mines, I had competed against the top 10 to 15 percent of the graduates of the high schools in Montana. I began to recover from a feeling of academic inferiority.

Academic knack, however, without flying aptitude wouldn't guarantee success in this program. In flight training you either passed or failed. Those who failed were "washed out." That sounded like you were rinsed, wrung, and hung out to dry like drop-seat longjohns. It really meant they gave you a one-way ticket to Great Lakes Naval Training Center near Chicago where they turned you into a deck-swabbing enlisted seaman. It was the dreaded elephants' graveyard for failed cadets.

The airport, a mile from town, had one runway, an undulating dirt strip scratched out of the sagebrush, alive with skittering jackrabbits, which adjoined another clearing where the airplanes were parked. Squat frame buildings served as the administration office, ready rooms, maintenance hangar, and refueling station. A faded windsock flapped lazily on a post near the runway.

The flight school operated seven Piper Cubs, one Waco biplane, and two others of obscure lineage. Its training staff was organized on a temporary paramilitary scheme set up by the Army Air Forces. The principal owner of the school, a short, grim, taciturn man, had the rank of major with Army Air Forces insignia, a leather jacket, and olive drab pants. The head instructor sported the bars of a captain, and the other instructors were first and second lieutenants. Despite this camouflage they were just civilian aviation buffs, "airport bums" or possibly crop dusters, dressed as military aviators. They could teach us the rudiments of flying and cull out those of us who couldn't adapt. We were supposed to salute these people, but enforcement was nonexistent mainly because neither they nor we knew how or when it was appropriate.

Marty, rumored to be the brother of a major league baseball player from a somewhat earlier time, became my instructor. In his mid-thirties, strong, silent, and prideful, Marty had, I sensed, a hidden envy of us beginners who were destined to go on to a level of flying and possible glory he could never attain. He would still be flying Piper Cubs when we were flying Grumman fighters from aircraft carriers.

Before my first flight, an event remembered vividly by all pilots, Marty showed me around a Piper Cub like a used car salesman pointing out the positive characteristics and minimizing the negative. This close inspection of the Cub, rather than reassuring me, heightened my apprehension. Nothing he said could change my impression that this was an exceedingly flimsy craft in which to trust my valuable life when out of contact with the ground. A better approach would have been to put me in the plane blindfolded.

I rode in the rear. Marty's broad back and the nose of the plane blocked the forward view. The herky-jerky motions while taxiing over the rough ground, the thumping of the little wheels on bumps, the thin snarl of its small engine (that must be why they called it a Cub), the birdlike flutter of the wings, and the chorus of rattles made me wonder why I had become involved in this activity.

Marty aimed this turkey into the wind. Holding the brakes, he revved up the engine and tested the magnetos one at a time. The engine stumbled on one magneto, which he ignored, mumbling what I took to be, "She'll be OK when she's a little warmer." He slowed the engine, released the brakes, and we lurched forward, gradually but bumpily gaining speed. The tail came up, lifted by the streaming air. I could see forward, and the rattles muted, then stopped. We were off the ground in the weakly supporting, untextured air.

The ground sped past, reminding me of my Chevy going downhill. In a few seconds, the apparent motion over the ground slowed to a pedestrian pace. Marty reduced engine power and it became surprisingly quiet. As we climbed, the ground seemed to stand still. My visual aspect had shifted 90 degrees. I now looked at the tops of objects instead of their sides. I had to learn to recognize familiar objects like trees again. From the ground a tree is a thing of beauty with limbs, trunk, and foliage in relief against the sky. From the air it's a green smudge, like a splat of spinach on the kitchen floor.

Susanville seemed startlingly small in the palm of the valley. As we labored for altitude, the green fields and blue gray sagebrush flooded out in all directions to the mountains, the ragged edge of the earth. We could peek into people's lives from above. Maybe I shouldn't have been looking. Vehicles crawled like ants on the roads. I felt detached from the earth, no longer part of it, hanging in a void, devouring a new world.

Marty had me follow through stick and rudder movements to feel their effects on the aircraft. "Jeez, take it easy, for Christ sake," he yelped. "The stick's not a damned baseball bat. Handle it as gently as you do your dick. The rudders ain't soccer balls, press 'em gently like you would a girl's tits."

He pointed out landmarks to memorize, fields that might be usable in case of engine failure, and how to recognize wind direction from rising smoke and swaying trees. Dazed by the enchanting flight, I had almost forgotten the behavior of the Cub on the ground. After the sharp jolt of first contact with the runway, the chorus of rattles took up where they had left off. This vehicle hated the ground. But she was aviator-friendly, really only a motorized glider with a large wing and small motor: slow, safe, and easy to fly.

Being out of contact with the ground is not a natural condition for man. Man evolved with his feet on the ground, essentially in a horizontal plane, bound by the law of gravity. To be where he moves in all planes, with gravity and other forces acting in ever-changing directions, requires that he abandon his sense of balance and accept the horizon in its place. When he makes a turn he should not feel the sensation of being thrown to the outside of the turn, as in a car. If he does, the turn is being poorly made; he is in a skid. He should have the sensation of being pressed into the seat. When the horizon is invisible, as in a cloud, the flier is in trouble unless he has the right instruments and knows how to use them.

On a flight a week later, while we were practicing landings, Marty stopped the plane on the runway, opened the door, and climbed out. "Take her around a couple of times," he said. The big moment had arrived, my first solo flight. I did as he said, but it was anticlimactic, a disappointment.

The Piper Cub was a "she." She despised surprising, abrupt movements and reacted sluggishly to them. She pretended to be weak and wanted to be coaxed with smooth, well-coordinated moves through sedate waltzes of wingovers and chandelles. Dives made her shudder, and climbing too fast made her stall, from which recovery could cost much hard-earned altitude and, if too near the ground, could kill the whole affair.

After a week at the airport, the major announced that three officers from the Army and the Navy were coming to inspect the school. He added, "I request that you naval cadets obtain khaki pants and shirts and black neckties to give some degree of uniformity to your group." While most of the Army men had khaki uniforms, jackets, and other flight clothing from some previous assignment, we had none. "To hell with that noise," Emmitt snorted. "If they want me in uniform, give me one and I'll wear it. Until then I'll look like what I am, a civilian." Most of us cobbled together at least a khaki shirt and necktie.

As part of the inspection, we posed for a group picture facing the administrative building. The photographer roosted on its roof. The airplanes formed a line behind us. In the front row stood our phony

Civilian Pilot Training, Susanville, California, fall 1942. Cadet Vernon is sixth from the far right.

major and his equally phony captain. To their left posed an Army officer with no jacket, a naval lieutenant in dress blues, and an Army first lieutenant, with dress jacket. We cadets and Army men in our highly varied garb, ranging from sport coats to white scarves and fleece-lined boots, were widely spaced in ranks to the rear of them, I presume to make us a more formidable-looking mass of fighting men. The photograph showed a motley crew reminiscent of multi-national Loyalist volunteer aviators taken during the Spanish Civil War somewhere in Andalusia. We looked dedicated and serious yet so pathetically inadequate it was hard for me to visualize any of us as naval officers fighting the fanatical Japanese in the Western Pacific.

Other than scheduled classes and flights, our time was our own. We played basketball at the high school, scouted the town for girls with no success, and routinely stopped at a popular local bar where questions about age were seldom asked. Compared to San Francisco or even Butte, Montana, Susanville was Dullsville.

A flight scheduled with Marty involved a search for him. During cold weather he snoozed like a hibernating bear in the instructors' ready room. During warm weather he sat on the stoop, a cigarette hanging from the corner of his mouth, while he read a newspaper or pulp magazine. When I approached, he took a last puff, stood up, stretched, pocketed his paper, and stomped out his cigarette. With me trailing him like a dog on a leash, we headed for the airplane. He seldom had anything to say to me until after the engine started and we began to taxi. I often wondered whether he made friends with anyone.

I had picked up a smattering of navigation and aerology and had logged thirty-five hours of flying time when the course ended: enough to feel comfortable in the air and confident that I would do OK flying. Bring on the regular Navy training.

2

Flying Endlessly in Piper Cubs

Back in San Francisco I waited for my orders, which instructed me to report to Alturas, California, for additional civilian pilot training. I resigned myself to more civilian flying from another hick town airfield. On my map, I found Alturas in the northeast corner of California, ninety miles north of Susanville. That meant retracing the route I had just traveled.

Alturas, less of a farm town and more of a cow town than Susanville, lay in a valley with low, wooded mountains nearby. The headquarters for the CPT instruction, a small, two-story building, faced the main street. A former elementary school, it contained an office, a classroom, and living quarters for the manager on the ground floor, and sleeping quarters and lavatory facilities for twenty cadets on the upper floor.

A middle-aged man ran the place, a former schoolteacher who acted like a drill sergeant, inspiring contempt in us. This training group included Bud and several other cadets I had known at Susanville. The rest had received their initial CPT training at other airfields scattered around northern California. We would fly Piper Cubs again and obtain some additional ground school.

Bud brightened when he saw me. "Whatcha doing in this hick town?" I asked. "I thought you were on your way to fight a war."

"Nah, I decided that war was bad and I would hide out here for the duration, flying endlessly in Piper Cubs. It looks like you're going to do it too. Let's check out the bunk room in this dump." It turned out to be a converted classroom with double bunks lining the walls. Showers and toilets were down the hall.

I had thought the airport at Susanville primitive but Alturas better fit that description. All surfaces usable by the aircraft were on volcanic soil cleared of sagebrush. A low frame building served as office and shelter from the weather for instructors and cadets. Aids to traffic control and navigation consisted of a tattered windsock near the landing strip. We were sliding downhill rather than rising to new heights.

My new instructor, Bill, was in his late twenties, had an athletic bearing and build, and was somewhat taller than I. He instructed well, but the program contained little that had not been covered at Susanville. We seemed to be wasting time here. He placed much emphasis on precision spins. He would say, "Do a two-revolution spin." I would line the plane up on a prominent landmark, using the rudders until it stalled, then kick the right rudder to start the spin. As it spun, I kept my landmark in sight as long as possible, watched it go past the nose the first time and waited for it to come into view the second time. About an eighth of a turn before it was dead ahead I would kick the left rudder to stop the spin, dump the stick forward into a dive, then add power to recover to level flight. He'd say, "That's pretty good but you came up short," or "You overshot a little." Then he'd demonstrate how it really should be done. I would nod my head in approval but knew he hadn't come any closer than I had.

Among the men I had not known at Susanville was a zippy cadet, Ken, who did much talking, liberally sprinkled with up-to-date clichés. He seemed excessively proud of his Rolex Oyster wristwatch and a Windsor knot in his necktie. He was the kind of city slicker who thought he could charm the farm boys from the Central Valley. His overuse of the pronoun "I" and his flood of know-it-all remarks irritated me. I had thought that having something to say was a mark of intelligence, but I learned that notion did not apply to Ken. When grades on examinations were posted, he was always at the middle or lower part of the list.

Ken prided himself on being an excellent pilot and a superior ladies man. He liked to describe in graphic detail his bedroom exploits at his previous training station. His specialty was orgasmic simultaneity, and trying to out-lie him was futile. It became obvious to everyone that he had no more success with the Alturas ladies than anyone else did, which is to say none. I earned his enmity by sniping tactlessly at him when he became intolerable. By chance, I served in the same units with him longer than with any other man in the Navy.

Between flights one afternoon, several of us were chatting on a graveled parking area when Bill, my instructor, joined us. We exchanged pleasantries and small talk until he focused his attention on me in what seemed to be good-natured joshing but had a challenging edge. He seemed to want to show his manliness and superiority in some way. Being an experienced scuffler, I good-naturedly shuffled about on the balls of my feet in a defensive mode. He grabbed my arms and began pushing me downward, which would certainly mean I would soon be on my knees, a position I would not accept without stiff resistance. Surprisingly, he persisted to a point where I was certain he wanted to wrestle and that I should make a move. I relaxed my resistance suddenly; he lurched forward and down, off balance, and his grip on my arms slipped. I broke loose and threw a headlock on him from which it would be difficult to escape without our rolling on the ground. He didn't struggle so I let him go. When he lifted his head his nose was bleeding from contact with my right thigh. He shot a hard look at me, fished a hankie out of his pocket, held it to his nose, and retreated. I had a sinking sensation: fear.

We had created an awkward situation but he could hardly report me for misconduct and still justify scuffling with a cadet. Nothing official was ever recorded regarding this incident except in my flight logbook. I discovered that he had retroactively checked in bright red ink the personality category "cocky" on all the flights I had taken with him.

By the time the three-week course ended, I had logged another twenty-five hours of flight time. I sold my car to a local farmer. The drill sergeant gave us our flight logbooks and put us on a bus to Reno where we were to catch a train to the Bay Area. While we waited far into the night for the train in Reno, I fell asleep sitting on a bench with my legs crossed. A sharp pain awakened me. Someone had given me a hotfoot that burned a hole in my shoe, sock, and big toe. I didn't wake up sooner because my foot was asleep and the pain didn't register until the burn was severe, the joke of a playful bunch of good fellows in need of a laugh.

Back in San Francisco, Mother greeted me with a big hug and a kiss. "How'd things go up in Alturas? Fun?" "Nah, more of the same old airplanes, just a holding pen until the naval training pipeline opens up. They kicked a cadet out of the program because he got airsick all the time. What's for dinner?"

In mid-January 1943, orders arrived directing me to report to the Ferry Building for transportation to the Naval Preflight School in Del Monte, California, the most dreaded and supposedly the toughest part of the training program.

I was ready.

3

Preflight School

Preflight really started when I kissed Mother good-bye. She looked brave but sad as I started down the stairs from her apartment carrying my overnight bag. She remained in the doorway until I looked back. She waved, but her heart didn't seem to be in it.

I stepped out of the building, which reeked of burnt toast and frying bacon, into the cool early morning fog and hunched my way to a small clot of people at a streetcar stop where I caught a plodding trolley that dropped me off at the Ferry Building. I joined a group of young men standing by a Navy bus with their backs to the drifting mist. Among them were several men I had known in CPT. Bud offered his hand, a smile, and "It's too late to quit now. We're off to Siberia." We boarded the bus as a yeoman with a clipboard called our names. The bus rolled south along the bay, out of the fog through San Jose and the green valley and mountains beyond. It crossed Steinbeck country around Salinas, where stooped men in straw hats and blue jeans labored in endless row crops. We curved around the southern end of Monterey Bay and stopped in a parking lot at the first-class Del Monte Resort Hotel, now a Navy preflight school.

The hotel's architect must have been inspired by the Spanish missions: tile roofs, beige walls, tile walkways, ornate doorways, everything except a bell tower, wooden cross, and swooping swallows. Imposing, mature trees shaded well-groomed expanses of lawn, an ideal spot for a honeymoon, but an unlikely looking place to train men for war. A greeting officer sent us to wait in the parking lot near a platoon sign. There, we joined several other cadets I had known at Susanville or Alturas and gathered around a burly ensign who introduced himself as "Schultz." While stragglers drifted in we could see cadet platoons drilling nearby, grim, stiff, precise, eyes straight ahead. I found it hard to believe, and a bit frightening, that we could be shaped up like that in a few weeks. A sobering experience must lie ahead of us. Schultz formed us into rough ranks and files and growled, "Follow me, men."

He led us to a wing of the hotel and the door of the platoon office where room assignments were posted. Thrust with me into a room were Ken, and four others I didn't know, two from Colorado, one from Reno, and one from Richmond. The boys from Colorado appeared to be certified clean-cut kids just out of high school. They seemed to feel the need to be mutually supportive in a hostile environment, a sort of circling-the-wagons. The cadets from Reno and Richmond were Italian but they could not have been more different. The Reno cadet was quiet and unassuming. The one from Richmond I remember only as "Pud" because that was his word to describe any person, thing, or action. I found it impossible to define the word in the manifold contexts in which he used it. It sounded obscene the way he said it, as though he was substituting it for some four-letter word. It seemed to be his all-inclusive generic obscenity. He appeared to be older than the rest of us; he looked tough, had dark skin, and talked out of the corner of his mouth. He came to think of himself as the "natural" leader of the platoon, covertly above Schultz, a kind of Sicilian godfather pose. At meals he contrived to sit at the head of the table, and he squeezed into the front row, center of our platoon picture, despite being taller than us shorties in that row. Ken began dazzling them with accounts of his accomplishments in the air and the bedroom. He wasted no charm on me because he knew my opinion of him.

Our room contained three double bunks and a desk. A bathroom and one closet served the six of us. The room reeked of mothballs from the newly unpacked white wool navy blankets. Until called out by platoons for the issue of uniforms, we learned how to make a bed Navy style. That proved to be a needlessly precise procedure that apparently was intended to teach us something about conformity and attention to details.

The issue of uniforms was anything but precise. I returned to my room loaded to the chin with clothes: khakis, whites, blues, and athletic gear, and a seabag to hold them. Skivvies were unisize, all large with string ties on the sides to adjust the waist. Some judicious swapping corrected most of the sizing errors. We sent our civilian clothes home. We would not wear their like again for years.

At the barbershop, the next stop, we obtained identical close-clipped haircuts. Stripped of our individuality, as expressed by our garb and hair, we superficially became more like all other cadets. My new appearance somewhat surprised me when I checked myself in a mirror. I felt strangely transformed and apprehensive about being dressed for entering another life, the nature of which I knew nothing.

Late in the afternoon that first day, we were ordered to muster for our first in-uniform formation, where the battalion's commanding officer briefed us on why we were there, the content of the program, and the schedule. We stood at attention until he shouted "At ease!" He seemed to be a well-balanced, thoughtful person, probably a former school principal, straining to be a no-nonsense military leader. He delivered a straightforward message. "You are here for three reasons: to learn what is required of a naval officer, acquire technical information that will be the foundation for integrating you into the naval flight program, and," with heavy emphasis, "be toughened physically for the demands of flying and any emergency you experience in combat."

He reminded us that failure to meet established minimum standards would be a threat to the well-being of our comrades in combat "Out There" and would mean dismissal from the program. He hoped none of us would fail to measure up. That said, we were told to prepare for reveille at 0600 hours, and he shouted, "Platoon Officers take charge. Dis . . . missed!" He was just another newly commissioned, ninety-day wonder. He and the other officers in the school had been no closer to Pearl Harbor, Coral Sea, or Midway than we had. It all seemed contrived and shallow, like a dress rehearsal by miscast actors.

Back in our room, Pud paraphrased his speech, "Listen to me you puds. I know what the pud I'm talking about. Our school will make an officer out of you by marching and running your puds off to see whether you can take it. If you can't take it we'll boot your pud out of here 'cuz 'Out There' in combat your buddies must rely on puds like you." Pud became our cynical alter ego. He saw through and sneered at Navy nonsense, posturing, and hypocrisy. He went too far in this, I felt. There must have been a sensible rationale behind much he sneered at.

We were finally in a military organization, the third battalion of six, each with 250 men that would bring the school to capacity. It would be our home for twelve weeks. The Navy had recruited the best staff available, mainly former schoolteachers and athletics coaches. I thought it reflective of the versatility of our society that these people were available. After ninety days of officer training they could pass on to us, who were destined to be the frontline fighters, much elementary information to prepare us for advanced training. Lacking on the staff were combat veterans, who were in high demand elsewhere.

Outlying buildings served as classrooms and sites for indoor athletics. We would learn soon enough that a nearby polo field and racetrack had been adapted for outdoor athletics. Within two days we were into a rigorous routine from 0600 to 2100 hours with scarcely a break. We marched as a platoon to and from every activity except athletics, when double-time was the pace to the athletic field, half a mile from the school.

Ensign Schultz, our platoon officer, as wide as he was tall, was a "jock" and not much else, like most of the athletic officers. He'd been commissioned straight off a professional football team where he'd fought in the trenches as a lineman. Despite officer preparatory training, he was friendly and gregarious, traits that could get a junior officer into trouble in the Navy, as I would later learn. The first time I saw him in shorts I was awed by his thighs, each of which had the girth of my torso. His lack of pretension and his willingness to share our grinding routine endeared him to us. Schultz saw that our platoon adhered to the schedule. He marched us to meals, classes, athletics, church, and led us in precision marching as part of the officer training. At some activities we were turned over to the specialists in charge. Schultz assisted them as needed. If it were a team sport, like soccer, he helped divide the platoon into teams, served as referee, and graded our performance.

The academic program consisted of two parts: officer training involved marching in close order, class instruction, and strict adherence to the military formalities of saluting, forms of address, details of dress, and shipboard terminology. Technical training related to aerology, aerodynamics, navigation, communications, and aircraft and ship identification.

Pud moaned about the ship and aircraft identification, "For the love of pud that Hun battleship *Tirpitz* has been holed up in a pudding Norwegian fjord for years. We're more likely to be skewered by a pudding Zulu than see that ship. And those pudding obsolete Italian bombers have been grounded for a year."

From the outset we found it hard to understand, even laughable to aspiring aviators, to contemplate the need for close-order marching or the need to know that in a ship the ceiling is the "overhead," the floor the "deck," the walls "bulkheads," and the stairs "ladders." In a ship, we were admonished, you don't go upstairs but "topside," and you don't go downstairs but "belowdecks." We learned that the proper response to an officer's order was "aye, aye, sir!" and the order "Bear a hand!" a salty way of saying "Hurry." This from a former schoolteacher, whom we dubbed "His Pudginess," who had never been to sea where he might have had to "bear a hand."

His Pudginess read to us "Rocks and Shoals," part of the Articles for the Government of the Navy that reminds all hands that the penalty for such acts as to "pusillanimously cry for quarter," is death, wording that dated back to the war of 1812. I wondered what it meant. It turned out it's an archaic, briny way of saying, "beg for mercy." He also showed us a film on avoiding venereal disease with the catchy title *She May Look Safe But. . . .* Pud groaned, "Who in the name of pud wrote that pud. What does that have to do with fighting a pudding war?" Information of that type was needed for us to feel the long tradition of the Navy and to fit quickly into the ship-navy on which aviation activities were dependent, but it seemed superfluous for men eager to get back to flying and on with the war.

The physical conditioning program occupied us for half of each day in competitive sports: soccer, American football, sprints and distance running, swimming, weight throwing, boxing, wrestling, and tumbling. They encouraged aggression. Presumably, you would make a better fighter if you could demonstrate aggression by beating the hell out of your comrades. Knowing we were being graded in each sport, we tried hard even when we might hurt a friend. Bud stung me with sharp punches when boxing, and I pinned him when wrestling. For every winner there had to be a loser.

They fed us in an enormous dining room that had been arranged to seat fifteen hundred cadets. At meal times we filed in, like novitiates in a religious sect, then stood at our tables silent as penitent monks, waiting for the order to be seated. The sound of that mob of hungry cadets rattling cutlery, eating, and talking was deafening. They fed us abundant, reasonably well-prepared food. After a short warning period, we were ordered to stand and march out. Despite the highly caloric diet, we began to lose weight.

In a moment of weakness I yielded to the urging of Ernie, a guy from the next room, and agreed to sing in the cadet choir. When we auditioned, I discovered he had a good voice and could read music and sing parts, none of which was true for me. I sang by ear and stood next to him to hear the notes he sang when singing parts. I could carry the melody and made a lot of noise when we did "Sky Anchors Away," the naval aviation song, and touching phrases from the mariners' hymn, which appealed for divine intervention "for those in peril on the sea."

Although the school demanded much, I remained confident that I would do well, having found CPT academic demands were far below those I had experienced in an engineering curriculum. The academic level at preflight school was the same as in CPT at Susanville. If it had been much more rigorous, Great Lakes would have received a flood of new enlisted seamen. I felt certain, also, that my years of participation in athletics from grade school through college would make me highly competitive in that part of the program. All things considered, it worked out as I expected. I took some hard lumps but I actually enjoyed much of it. Others despaired.

Pud would return from an afternoon of running, jumping, rope climbing, and wrestling, flop on his bunk, and groan, "I ache from the soles of my pudding feet to my scalp. These mothah pudders are trying to kill me." Pud, a scofflaw, had trapped himself in a system he hated but could not openly resist for fear of the severe penalties. He regressed to furtive shirking and ridicule.

My confidence took a severe hit when I discovered that I had earned failing grades reading blinker, Morse code sent by a flashing light. I could wash out of the program despite doing well in all other activities. The reasoning here went: If you can't read blinker you must not be able to concentrate; therefore you can't fly an airplane effectively. I did so poorly reading it that I had to attend a special class with some forty other cadets from our battalion for additional practice and testing. Despite my short attention span for blinker, I eventually passed with a minimum score. No one I knew ever had an occasion to read blinker during the war.

I had a friendly competition going for high grades in ground school with Cadet Martin. He was a tall handsome man who had two years of college and routinely placed among the top three in academic work. Although his legs appeared to be well developed, he couldn't jump and could run only slowly. Special attention and examinations determined that although his muscles were well developed, his Achilles and hamstring tendons were too weak to sustain vigorous exercise without pain. He dropped from the program, destination Great Lakes. With his intelligence, he surely would get into another program and get a commission.

Offsetting the disappointment of losing Martin was the staying power of obnoxious Ken. To watch him hurdle, run, and lumber through the obstacle course or any other activity requiring speed and agile footwork wrung sympathy even from me. Still his mismatched legs, one a third wider than the other, proved to be strong and durable. He marched well, even at double time, and he turned out to be a good swimmer. That helped to compensate for the low grades he received in other sports. He met the minimum standards and stayed up with the rest of the platoon. Despite my dislike for him, I couldn't help but admire his dogged determination to succeed.

The time required to run the obstacle course measured our progress in physical conditioning. The toughest obstacle, an eight-foot-high wall, proved a nightmare for many cadets. To top the wall you had to sprint at it, strike one foot on its face for a momentary foothold, jump, grasp its top, and pull yourself up and over. I had watched dozens do it that way before a lean, wiry athlete from a Utah college made his run. He had a reputation for being a great athlete, so I watched closely. He started like everyone else but his push-off from the wall lifted him high. He yanked himself up with both hands, rotated his body to a horizontal position and shifted to a one-hand vault, clearing the top by a couple of feet and landed running on the other side. He had the fastest time in the battalion. Pud muttered, "That mothah pudder makes us look like cold pud."

Pud let it be known that he was a dangerous man to cross and a street brawler of some experience. That pose was likely to attract negative reactions among associates, and it did. During one of our boxing sessions, he was matched against a cadet of seemingly mild demeanor. Within a minute, a sharp right to the chin flattened Pud. He lay there a few seconds, raised himself on his elbows, shook his head, and got to his feet. The instructor stopped the match. His opponent smirked, but I never let on that I had seen Pud go down. I noted no change in his attitude after that. He kept pudding this and pudding that.

One day I took a shortcut to the Navy exchange through the officers' parking lot. There I noticed a distinctive, pale blue Chevrolet sedan I was certain I'd seen a hundred times before. It had a Montana license with "5" as the first number, showing its home as Helena, where I had gone to high school. It had to belong to Hank Secrest, my coach there.

I looked into the windows but learned nothing. How to get in touch with him? I dug a scrap of paper out of my pocket and wrote him a short note. As I inserted it under the windshield wiper a voice said, "Excuse me, cadet, may I help you?" I looked up and saw old Hank. Surprised, he was no more prepared to manage our changed relationship than I. In almost any other circumstances I would have addressed him as Hank, shaken his hand, and perhaps given him an affectionate pat on the shoulder. Should a cadet do that to a senior officer? I played it safe, saluted, and said, "Hello, Mr. Secrest. How nice to see you again."

He saluted, "Jim, I didn't know you were here. How are things going?"

"Not bad; it's not as tough as I expected."

He shrugged, "You shouldn't have any trouble with the athletic program and your going to the School of Mines must make the classroom work a cinch."

I felt uncomfortable making small talk with an officer, even old Hank Secrest. "I'm on a tight schedule," I said. "I'd better get going. It's great seeing you again." I saluted.

He returned the salute hesitantly and said, "Thanks, good to see you again, good luck."

I thought it odd and even sad to see our behavior so restrained. The Navy had erected an invisible barrier between us and to some degree dehumanized us. Regrettably, I never saw him again.

Most cadets found athletics the most demanding part of the program. The strain of hours of strenuous exercise was to a considerable degree reduced by the cool weather. I finished the program in excellent physical condition and good spirits, but many were drained physically and emotionally, and highly resentful.

Toward the end of preflight training, we could request flight training at any of three primary training stations listed in our order of preference. The stated intention was to reward performance at preflight by sending the highest achieving cadets to the station of their choice. Moans and cheers greeted the list of assignments when posted. I cheered. I received my first choice, Livermore Naval Air Station in the San Francisco Bay Area. Pud got Livermore also.

One last demand fell on us before leaving the Del Monte: a graduation ceremony. On a sunny day in the early afternoon we showered, shaved, shined shoes, and brushed the white lint from our blue wool uniforms, all the while cursing the white blankets from which it came.

The ceremony site, a vast parking lot at the front of the hotel, had a stage fitted out with flags, bunting, seats for high-ranking officers and visiting dignitaries, and a public address system. The station band was seated off to one side, and the other five battalions stood in ranks facing the stage. Visiting family members, in a holiday mood, stood on the grass around the perimeter of the parking lot.

As the graduating battalion, we mustered at the side of the hotel. When the band began to play Sousa's rousing "Washington Post March" our commanding officer called, "Attention! Right face! Forward harch!" and off we marched to occupy the place of honor before the stage. The reason for all that precision marching drill became clear. I had to admit that as we marched I felt a thrill along my spine, and my heart beat faster. This, I realized, was part of the Navy attitude training that would make me willing to give all for my country.

The program started with the national anthem and a prayer by the chaplain. As we stood at parade rest, my mind recorded none of the blather spoken by the guests and the commanding officer of the school; my thoughts were of my family nearby. Dad had come all the way from Montana for this event, as well as to visit his three daughters and nurture his fading hope for a reconciliation with Mother.

Suddenly it ended. Sousa's "Stars and Stripes Forever" sprang up from the band and again our battalion commander took charge: "Attention! Left face! Forward harch!" and marched us back to our starting point, where he shouted a long-awaited "Platoon leaders take charge. Dis . . . missed!"

My family and I found each other in the crowd, the first time we had been together since 1936, when my sister Janice had moved to Los Angeles to enter nurses' training. My sisters, Myrl, Janice, and Rosemary, all older than I, were accompanied by their husbands, two of whom were in the service, stationed in the Bay Area. Being the center of attention after twelve weeks of isolation pleased me.

Dad had the good sense to rent a room in a hotel and bought some whiskey and mix. We helped him consume it. I watched Mother and Dad; they were distant, neutral, and polite to each other. That boded ill for their future relationship. As always, their

Del Monte Preflight School, California, winter 1942–43. Cadet Vernon is in the first row, third from left.

private feelings were not on display when their kids were present.

We reminisced, toured the seashore, and snapped photographs of us in several combinations. Time crawled through what turned out to be an awkward afternoon until my liberty ended and my family had to return to San Francisco. I parted from them in a somber mood that not even my cheerful sisters could dispel.

The graduation ceremony struck me as too much show for men who had barely started on a program that many would not complete; more pretentious, in fact, than any other stage of training, including being commissioned and being designated "naval aviator." I would realize later that the ceremony was indicative of the contrast between the tradition-bound ship-Navy of preflight and the more relaxed air-Navy we were about to enter. Pud grumbled when the ceremony had ended, "This is all plain old bullpud. Pud preflight school."

I'm surprised that I've remembered so much about preflight school, since it was largely extraneous to becoming an aviator, something to be endured, an obstacle, a test to be passed before being awarded the prize—the opportunity to become a flying officer. Those memories are disconnected, like snapshots in an album. I remember the sounds: reveille, running feet on the deck and stairs, shouted commands, band music, marching cadences shouted in unison, muffled curses and grunts, droning lectures, Morse code clatter, taps. And the sights: marching men, blinking lights, needles, flags, gold braid, sweating bodies, hurdles, tired eyes, tears. And the feelings: winning, losing, anger, disgust, impatience, slippery bodies, stinging blows, hard ground, aching muscles, tired feet. The events I remember most clearly are those in which I personally experienced success or failure, and those humorous, courageous, or ugly.

Yet memories of men rekindle events, which in turn trigger a wide range of feelings: Pud's colorful and humorous insights and irreverences pointing out the flaws in the system and providing us relief from growing tensions. Ken, he of the neat necktie, getting us past a white glove inspection by cleaning crevices in our bunk frames that were the first place the inspecting officer put his glove. Ernie, the singer, pushing me into the choir and the pleasure of music, remnants of which still, uncalled, run through my mind. Schultz, our burly and benign leader demonstrating a required exercise and failing. And Bud's steady temperament and excellence in all sports.

With the last race run, wall climbed, push-up strained, and test passed, tension in the battalion gradually faded; smiles replaced deadpans; jokes, gripes; laughs, curses; and sympathy, disinterest as we looked to the future, like mountaineers resting in a shady spot, gathering strength for a precipitous upland ahead.

A few days later, Pud and I, along with other cadets, left the bullpud of preflight school behind and rode a Navy bus to Livermore Naval Air Station. We would be back to flying again, this time Navy flying.

4

On the Brink of Washing Out

The air station, in a valley between San Francisco Bay and the Central Valley, occupied a square mile surrounded by agricultural land and rolling hills still green from the winter rains. The ranch buildings and trees that had once stood there had been leveled to make way for a square, asphalt landing area and rows of gray, ugly frame buildings surrounded by a high chain-link fence, reminiscent of low-security penal institutions.

The bus dumped our seabags and us at the administration building, where a yeoman checked us in. He led us, our spirits lifted by the sight and roar of airplanes, to the enlisted men's barracks we were to occupy, a two-story structure that could house forty or more men in double bunks on each level. A community lavatory with rows of showers, wash basins, and toilets without doors serviced each floor.

I was a card in a great deck that after each game was shuffled and dealt into new combinations by some anonymous hand. I knew only Pud among the cadets who were dealt with me into that barracks, which would be my home for the next three months. Pud held himself aloof from the flurry of moving in, leaning against a doorjamb, chewing a toothpick, and smirking. I nudged him and asked how he liked his new home.

He grumbled out of the corner of his mouth, "These mothah pudders think we're sardines. We'll have as much privacy as a pudding canary in a pet store." He spoke the truth in his obscene way. Privacy had been banned from our lives. In its place were airplanes. We were in a hive of yellow airplanes that endlessly took to the air, circled, landed, crawled on the asphalt, and filled our ears with their growling. That night they became noisy fireflies flashing red, green, and white lights and exhaling blue red gas, a visible challenge and a portent of what lay ahead for us. I reminded myself that cadets in those planes had come from preflight only a few weeks earlier. All that had gone before now seemed trivial.

I drew a bunk within an arm's length of five other cadets, one in the bunk above and four in adjacent bunks. Pud had a bunk nearby. We began talking about hometowns, CPT, preflight. How did you like the program so far? The answers were the hometown was the best, CPT fun, and preflight lousy. Preflight had been such a recent, rough experience, we tended to exaggerate the difficulties. All seemed satisfied to have survived it. To me, preflight had been a hazing.

We were now among men who had passed the same demanding tests and had the same objectives; this drew us together as a definable group of mavericks. We were yet to be branded as officer or enlisted man, and were shunned by both groups. We knew only cadets.

Barracks living was a remarkably orderly and efficient system that had evolved over millennia in the military: bunks and lockers in precise rows; personal gear stored in specified ways; beds made according to rules; and the routine rigid. Grooming, dress, and behavior were defined to make us all the same. It was a new experience to sleep so closely packed with men in the same room. As lights-out approached, a flurry of activity began, last-minute showers and tooth-brushing, breakup of card games and bull sessions, and slamming of locker doors. Lights-out marked a gradual drop in chatter level punctuated by outbursts of smart-ass anonymous shouts, hoots in response, and ripples of laughter. These gave way under persistent "pipe-downs" and "knock-it-offs." Soon a murmur of deep breathing, grunting, farting, snoring, and muffled bedspring creaks drifted over us.

This group of men, full of high spirits and horseplay, could have come from my high school graduating class. A few would become transitory Navy friends. The chance of bunk assignment put me next to a thin, blond, somewhat stooped cadet from Los Angeles named Paul. He had a friendly, sincere, and questioning face, as though life and the Navy were complex beyond his comprehension; a feeling common, to some degree, to all, but we tried not to let it show. He followed the rules but never got them exactly right. He neither stood nor marched straight and never exactly in step. However, Paul made no gross errors and did well in classes and athletics and passed all his flight checks, just a little out of sync. He was dependable and comfortable to be with, like an old house cat. In return, I gave him companionship and civility.

Then there was the Lodi Kid, a farmer from the Central Valley near Lodi who liked to drink and chase women and was not above crowing about his conquests. He was tall, blond, and brawny, with a broad face, large feet, and strong bony hands.

"He got those hands from yanking carrots, picking cotton, and pitching hay," Paul said. "Those feet of his are deformed from kicking clods."

"Yeah, you're skinny from breathing smog all your life, Smoggy Paul," the Lodi Kid sneered back.

The nicest cadet in the barracks was a Mormon from Utah; too nice, I thought, for flying in combat. He seemed out of place in a program training men to kill other men. He smiled a lot, habitually cast down his eyes, and his soft voice made me think he agreed with me even when he said "no." We nicknamed him Brigham. He didn't let on when something irritated him but simply turned the other cheek. He wanted to be accepted as one of the gang but couldn't hang around when we spouted obscenities and religious epithets. The Lodi Kid took perverse pleasure in making him uncomfortable by relating blow-by-blow accounts of real or imagined bedroom exploits. "Those rosebud nipples were delicious but it was time to dip my wick in the honey slit." Brigham fled. I envied his tranquility and sensed that he lived on a higher moral plane than the rest of us. I found it easy to fit in with these men.

We trained in the Stearman N2S, a biplane with two open cockpits, affectionately known as the "Yellow Peril," the plane in which all naval aviation cadets began training during World War II. We would all remember them, the lowest common denominator, and the exhilaration of flying in an open cockpit. Yellow fabric covered

The Stearman N2S, a biplane with two open cockpits, was affectionately known as the "Yellow Peril." It was the plane in which naval aviation cadets began training during World War II.
U.S. Naval Institute

framing and controls of great strength. No aerial maneuver could cause a mechanical failure or a landing that more than flattened a tire or scraped a wing tip. A reliable 250-horsepower radial engine drove a wooden propeller. They had excellent stability at low speed, a characteristic needed for training naval aviators to land on an aircraft carrier, certainly the safest plane we would ever fly.

Within two days, we were flying and attending ground school, a half-day each. My first experience flying in an open cockpit seemed downright insecure: being held in the airplane by only a seat belt, a feeling that escalated to terror when flying upside down. But to know more intimately the air that hissed across my face and fluttered my sleeves made flying more birdlike, a feeling absent in enclosed cockpits.

About half the instructors were civilian pilots, voluntary reservists (USNR-V), mostly men in their thirties and forties who would remain instructors for the duration and then return to civilian life. They had no military training, and it showed in their laid-back attitude, dress, and bearing. They lived off the station with their wives and kids, like civilian nine-to-fivers, undemanding and sympathetic toward us cadets.

The others were naval aviator graduates from Pensacola or Corpus Christi who had been removed from the track that would have taken them to combat aircraft and the fleet. Instead they had been sent back to teach beginners like us, leaving behind any dreams of adventure and glory. They were young and dissatisfied with their lot. Most had lost hope of ever flying fighters or other high-powered aircraft. Their bitterness surfaced by being demanding in the air and difficult to satisfy on check flights. We were wary, even afraid of them.

Each flight took me from the miniramas of the ground to the panoramas of the sky. The ugly details of the earth were lost in the wraparound screen of sky, clouds, horizon, and land and sea. I felt suspended, unmoving or slowly crawling, a sensation that became stronger as altitude increased. As the earth appeared to stand still beneath me, my thoughts sometimes wandered to the wonder of flight and the mysteries of all that was spread before me and how little I understood any of it.

I saw but a small patch of Mother Earth's vast skin, mountains, just wrinkles on her face, and the valley but an engaging dimple, the distant sparkling bay a tear or perhaps sweat on her brow. I learned to love her—and flying—more, for each flight gave me another visual embrace with the sweetest sight on earth, our earth itself.

At first, flying gave me the best possible sense of landscapes, but an incomplete feeling nagged me. The view was static, more like a landscape photograph. Something was missing. I had a broad view of the earth but no intimacy with it. To know a landscape, I realized, I must know its reality in all its forms: feel the texture of its soil, hear wind stir the trees and rain pelt the grass, and smell its flowers and new-mown hay. But the roar of the engine kept me in touch with reality. It held me aloft, but only for a finite time measured by the amount of gasoline in the tank. Running out of gas in an automobile is inconvenient; running out of gas in an airplane is life threatening. Early on in my flying experience, I learned to remind myself that a life-threatening situation due to an empty gas tank was an avoidable error. My best friend in the sky was a full tank of gasoline; my worst enemy, the unseen aircraft flying near me.

The Navy flight program assumed that we had never flown before. We flew ten hours of familiarization with an instructor in the front cockpit whose main purpose was to teach us to land Navy style, tail down in a stall as the wheels touch the ground, get the feel of the aircraft in standard maneuvers, and learn safety procedures. "To land right you gotta drag your ass in the dust," the Lodi Kid said. I dragged my ass in the dust and survived that part with only one partial ground loop that scraped a wing tip, and passed the first flight check with no difficulty.

I knew something was up when the Lodi Kid sauntered into the barracks with that certain look and said, "I've got something for you half-assed aviators."

"OK, what's on your mind," Paul said.

"Have you heard about the instructor at a station out in Kansas?"

"OK, Lodi, let's have it. I hope you don't scare off Brigham."

"No, no, he'll like this. There was this instructor who had a special way to force timid cadets to make their first landing. In flight, he would duck down and remove the stick in his cockpit, which, you know is attached to the same controls as the stick the cadet has, wave it to make sure the cadet was watching, throw it over the side, and tell the cadet to land. It worked like a charm until a cadet obediently copied him, ducked down and came up with his stick, waved it and tossed it away. The smart-ass instructor damn near crapped his britches and bailed out, but the smirking cadet landed the airplane.

"How'd he do it?" I asked.

"He'd secretly brought a spare stick with him."

You don't expect us to believe that, do you?" said Paul. "Hell, it's no more believable than some of your sex stories."

"I swear to God. I heard it from a cadet as honest as Brigham here."

With the easy part of the syllabus completed, I had to learn to land within a small circle marked on a field, the Navy way, tail down in a stall to catch an arresting wire as if I had a hook and were landing on a carrier. Two techniques were taught, slipping to increase the rate of descent, and making an S-turn on the approach to lose altitude by shortening or lengthening the glide path. It didn't seem very difficult. We were assigned to practice on one of several outlying dirt fields. After the required hours of instruction and practice, the dreaded flight check came. The check pilot gave me a "down," a serious setback. I had earned that down. For some reason I couldn't slip the plane worth a damn. I couldn't face my friends. I skipped evening chow and skulked off to my bunk where I lay staring at the springs of the bunk above. It meant that I would have to take another check ride the next day with a different check pilot. He gave me an "up." That evened the score. The fateful third check brought another "down." I could wash out and go off to Great Lakes unless an advisory board gave me additional flight time and another two check flights. My failed landings played and replayed in my mind. It baffled me. I tried not to think about how I would explain my failure to my family.

When the board met, a yeoman ushered me into a small classroom where three senior officers were seated in students' chairs. They had a folder that I presumed held my service record covering my preenlistment exams, CPT, preflight school, and results so far at Livermore, that I hoped they had reviewed in advance.

The senior board member, an easygoing senior lieutenant, began. "Stand at ease, Cadet." I stood at military ease but my mind and nerves were at attention. "We would like to know whether you want to continue flight training?"

"Yes sir, I do very much. More than anything I've ever done."

"Why do you think you got those two downs?"

"I can't explain it. Just had a couple of off days, I guess. Most of the time things like that come easily to me, which you can see from the high scores I got at preflight school."

"Do you feel fear when you fly?"

"No, sir, but I know it can be dangerous and don't take any chances."

They whispered among themselves and looked at my record and me while I stood trying to look very determined and military. They nodded at each other. The lieutenant looked me in the eye, "If we give you another chance would you want a different instructor?"

If I said "yes" it would sound like blaming the instructor, a contradiction of my lame "bad day explanation."

"No, I have a good instructor. I wouldn't want to change."

They ordered me to wait outside for what turned out to be the longest ten minutes of my life before the lieutenant came out and said, "We have decided to give you another six hours of flight time, three hours with your instructor and three hours solo." He smiled, "Good luck."

I breathed again. This reprieve from a death sentence meant imprisonment until I had earned a pardon by passing two check flights. When I met my instructor again for additional training he looked puzzled and asked, "What happened? I was certain you would pass the check." I shrugged and hung my head, couldn't meet his eyes; I had let him down.

Until the time for the checks, I thought through multiple times all aspects of hitting the circle, altitude, distance from the target, airspeed, engine RPM, wind direction, even what I would eat for breakfast.

The first check flight was with Dobson, one of the older, fatherly pilots, a USNR-V who had a special interest and talent for helping cadets who were in trouble in the flight program. He smiled and laid a firm hand on my shoulder, "Let's go out and see how you can do. It's a great day for flying, sun's bright and the winds calm. I've checked your records. This should be a cinch for you." As we walked to the airplane, he asked, "Jim, where's your hometown?"

"San Francisco, right now." I relaxed a little. He continued in that vein as we flew to an outlying field. When we landed he climbed out and said, as he stood on the wing, "Take it easy and good luck." Take it easy, for God's sake, when I was taut as a strut wire with my aviation career at stake?

I had to make six attempts to land in the circle, three by slipping and three by S-turning. I hit the circle four times and was close twice. He gave me an "up." On the ground after the check he smiled, shook my hand, and said, "You did a great job. I knew you could do it."

"Thanks, Mr. Dobson."

The next day I went for my final check ride. Dobson flew with me to the field. En route he said, "Just do it like yesterday, and everything will be OK." The check pilot, a naval aviator, stood on the field. Dobson climbed out, gave me a pat on the shoulder, winked, climbed to the ground, and waved reassuringly. I hit the circle on the first four attempts and the fifth was nearly perfect. What a change from some of my previous attempts. I couldn't believe that I could do it again, but the sixth was perfect. I kept the plane on the ground, and Dobson got in for the ride back. As we took off, he looked back at the check pilot standing at the edge of the target circle. My eyes followed his. The check pilot gave a high thumbs-up signal. A wave of relief and exhilaration spilled over me. I had earned a pardon. There would be no confession of failure to my family.

Standing on the brink of washing out and staring down the slippery slope into the abyss of enlisted anonymity had subdued and sobered me. I wanted to fly and felt I had an aptitude for it, but I still couldn't explain why I had failed that first check flight. Perhaps my aptitude was not as great as I believed; perhaps I was just cocky, as that CPT instructor had said. Such thoughts did little to encourage me as I entered the most difficult part of the program for most cadets: aerobatics.

"Aerobatics is flying like an acrobat," said a senior instructor who briefed us. "Many aerobatic stunts have no practical application in any part of aviation except the military. Even we in the military have little need for a snap roll, slow roll, loop, precision spins and stalls, and variations of these. Their main purpose is to familiarize you with the capabilities and limitations of the aircraft, and of yourselves. It also prepares you for unusual situations and attitudes that you might encounter in combat. And finally, it gives you a feeling of oneness with the airplane and makes you comfortable in any attitude, despite the interplay of gravitational, centrifugal and centripetal forces, and weightlessness acting in combination." He concluded, "Eventually it will teach you to fly by instinct, thus freeing your mind for other activities."

Pud translated all this for us. "You puds are going to learn some tough pudding stuff you will never use and get your puds booted out of the program if you don't learn it good. We'll try to tear you puds apart to see if you can take it."

The aerobatics training syllabus required that I learn several standard stunts, loops, slow rolls, snap rolls, chandelles, Immelmanns, and spins, to a fair degree of precision. After an hour's instructional flight on a stunt or two, I spent three or four flights practicing them. The instructor would then test me and introduce me to other stunts. Once I recovered from the shock of being subjected to attitudes and forces never before experienced, I found aerobatics exhilarating. Anyone who likes carnival rides would love aerobatics.

Occasionally, an instructor would deviate from the syllabus, probably out of boredom or a desire to show me that there were tricks more difficult than those required. They performed some outrageous maneuvers that put unbelievable strain on the aircraft and its occupants. One instructor specialized in an outside loop. He began by pushing the nose down, but instead of pulling it up and going around, he pushed it into a vertical dive and then past vertical until the plane was inverted. At this point, gravity and centrifugal force were trying to tear me from the plane. I hung on like a leech, wishing I had double-checked my seat belt and thinking of the thousands of feet of empty air between the ground and me. At the bottom of the loop, hanging upside down, I could see the horizon again but with the earth above and the sky below until we were in a vertical climb; the strain on the seat belt decreased. The plane slowed and staggered into level flight, putting the horizon back where it belonged, with the sky on top.

An outside slow roll was another belt-hanger that made me airsick when an instructor, without warning, did three in succession. I gave him the "sick" signal and we landed with my breakfast still where it belonged. I would have to be bored stiff with flying before I'd try either of those stunts. They repelled me as a waste of courage and heroic impulse and as just plain irresponsible. I should have a good reason before I took such risks, and should avoid applying maximum engine power or strains on a plane in flight unless it was necessary. Those were the conditions under which something mechanical would fail.

When check time came I felt ready but apprehensive. Several cadets I knew had received "downs," but this time I received an "up." My self-confidence flooded back.

One day, all cadets at the station were assembled to hear a presentation by a great aviator, someone I'd never heard of, Joe Foss, then the top American ace of the war, with twenty-six planes shot down over the Solomon Islands. Joe, a Marine, carried himself like an athlete as he strode back and forth across the stage.

His presentation rambled without props except for a logbook that he glanced at to check dates and types of aircraft he had shot down. Like all aviators, he used his hands to illustrate the position of his plane and the targeted enemy when he "squeezed off a shot" or "gave him a squirt." He spoke code names for Japanese planes—Zero, Kate, Betty, and others we had learned in preflight school—as he knocked them out of the air, that made us feel like we were part of the in-group. His modest attitude about his accomplishments made a good impression on the audience of fledgling aviators. He gave a low-key pep talk near the end and answered a few questions from the cadets.

It was as close as any of us had been to a genuine war hero. I don't doubt that some in our group elected to go into the Marine Corps because of that presentation. It reinforced my desire to fly fighters, to do it alone, perhaps the same impulse that propelled the knights-errant of history.

Every weekend I saw cadets escorting their hometown sweethearts around the station. These girls were always chaperoned by their mothers. Pangs of envy gnawed at me because I had no girlfriend who cared enough about me to visit. I rationalized that I had never lived long enough in one place to establish a close relationship with a nice girl and her family. Two years was the longest I had lived in one place since the sixth grade.

Things heated up when I met a nurse, Susan, in San Francisco and began dating her regularly. She had natural beauty and manners. She needed no heavy makeup, no phony poses or conversation. You had to take her as she was, or not at all. I became fond of her. She seemed to like me, but it went no deeper than that, not very romantic. My initial fantasy of a conquest was dashed by her rigid schedule at the hospital where she trained and by her conservative drinking habits. When I came in from another disappointing evening with Susan, the Lodi Kid, standing bleary-eyed at a urinal, grunted, "Did your stiletto fit Susan's scabbard?" From my look, he knew the answer. I crawled into my bunk, stiff and aching, and tried to sleep.

Liberty meant a trip to San Francisco to date Susan and visit my family. My mother and sisters could always find a place for me to stay overnight in their apartments. I borrowed Jumbo, their car, a 1928 Chevy sedan, to prowl about the city with Cliff, an old friend from the School of Mines, who was stationed there in the Army. Nice girls were scarce, so we wasted much effort on the other kind in carousing and bar hopping.

One Saturday morning a messenger from the station gate announced that I had a visitor. As I neared the gate I could see a soldier leaning against the guard shack talking to the guard. He turned as I walked up. It was Cal, my high school buddy from Nevada. His grin said it all about warm, lasting friendship. It felt good to see his short, wiry frame, shake his hand, and hug his rock-solid shoulders. "It's great to see you again, Jimmy; its been a long time. I came to find out what you're up to."

He eyed the rows of Yellow Perils. "First off, I want to see the airplanes." We climbed onto the wing of one. "Can I get in?" he asked.

"Sure." He scrambled in with the agility of a monkey, looked at the instruments, and pushed the stick around. I yelped like my CPT instructor, "Not so damn hard; it's not a baseball bat, for god's sake. Handle it like you do your dick."

With my expert instruction, he maneuvered the controls in simulated turns, dives, and landings. When I finally coaxed him out of the plane, he said, "Jimmy, you're into a good deal; I'd like to get into flying."

"That can wait," I said. "Right now I want to beat you again at table tennis. Just follow me."

"That'll be the day. I can still beat you using my left hand."

With that disagreement settled indecisively again, I slicked up and we headed to San Francisco. On the bus, I kidded him about the time he shot a pheasant out of season, then a few minutes later shot a hole in the roof of my dad's car. He laughed, "That was nothing compared to the time you almost got us caught using your Oklahoma credit card at that construction site." They were laughing matters now and the glue of friendship.

In San Francisco, he got hugs and kisses from my mother and sisters. It had taken seven years for our friendship to mature to this depth of feeling and understanding. Could I ever develop that great a friendship with any of the dozens of men that wandered in and out of my life in the Navy? That liberty reminded me that, besides flying, there were good times without chasing women and carousing. Someone once observed that booze is a substitute for sex on the frontier; it also plays that role in many military situations.

Night flying was the final trial. Anecdotes that exaggerated the hazards did nothing to ease the prospect. One that went around concerned a cadet who, startled by engine exhaust flames, thought the plane was on fire and bailed out. Another story that titillated us concerned a cadet who was instructed to follow the white taillight of the plane that took off just before him. That taillight continued in a straight line until the cadet ran out of gas and bailed out. He had been following a star.

Darkness made everything more difficult, even finding the right plane on the tarmac while avoiding the spinning propellers. Visual cues of distance and the relationships among objects on the ground were erased. When taxiing, the only guides were colored lights marking taxi strips and runways. Since the engine blocked the view ahead, I had to make S-turns. At the takeoff position, two lines of converging lights marked the edges of the runway, a path to the stars. A dim horizon would not appear ahead until well into my takeoff run, which amounted to steering the plane between the runway marker lights. At first, I could see them by glancing right and left. Once the tail was lifted by the flowing air, the nose came down and both lines of light were visible. I split the distance between them by riding the rudder pedals. My newly gained flying instincts and feel for the airplane told me when it wanted to fly. I eased back on the stick and the plane left the ground. My old friend, the horizon, was skulking in the distance as though reminding me how important it was to my safety in the air. I rose and flew between two night skies: the familiar starry one above and the black one below dotted by constellations of man-made stars.

The instruments glowed in a black pit, indicating only a fraction of the information they did in daylight. On either side the running lights were hypnotically bright and seemingly detached. The engine exhaust stack, that in daylight emitted only heat waves, had become a roaring blowtorch.

I was in the air with several other cadets to make a series of landings, the most difficult part of the flight. When my turn came, I lined up with the runway, a trough between the lights, narrow, black, and of unseeable depth. As I passed between the lines of lights, some notion of my height above the runway could be gained by glancing at them. I flared out and stalled the plane. It settled into the trough and found bottom by itself.

It shocked me the first time I saw a friend's bunk empty, his gear gone, bedding folded and stacked on the mattress, and his locker half open. Pud saw me staring at it, "That pud took a trip to Great Lakes; he's one of the lucky pudders."

Others followed him, Pud included. When leaving he said, "Pudding night flying is lingering suicide. It's not for this pud. I'd rather be a live seaman than a dead pudding pilot." I would miss Pud and his pudding cynicisms. He and the others exited my life as completely as if they had fallen from the face of the earth. They were now inferior beings because they didn't fly.

My stay at Livermore neared its end. The hills that had been green when I arrived had long since faded to brown. My next stop would be Pensacola or Corpus Christi. Any doubts I had of completing the program and getting those wings of gold and a commission had been blunted by success at Livermore. I felt that I was well adapted to flying and that I would make as good an officer as most of the cadets. The Navy had much time and treasure invested in me; it was in their best interest to get me through the program and on to fighting the war. I realized that I now flew instinctively. I had become an integral part of the airplane, making us a complete flying organism. It seemed now not much different than driving a car.

During that summer of 1943 while I flew at Livermore and caroused in San Francisco, Allied forces in the Pacific had stopped the Japanese in New Guinea and their threat to Australia. Hard fighting was in progress as our forces pushed north through the Solomon Islands to neutralize Rabaul. In the European Theater, Allied forces had invaded and secured North Africa and were fighting in Sicily and Italy. The Battle of the Atlantic against Nazi submarines had turned dramatically in our favor. Letters from high school and college friends reported that some of our schoolmates had fallen in the fighting.

I received orders to Corpus Christi, Texas, for advanced training. In late August 1943, in high spirits, fifty other cadets and I boarded several troop railway sleeper cars at Livermore. Rows of bunks two or three high occupied most of the space in the car, leaving a narrow aisle for access to the bunks and toilet.

In the cool, coastal climate of the San Francisco Bay Area, dress blues had been the uniform-of-the-day, so we began the trip in them. As the train rolled south and east informality of dress increased. We were soon in skivvies playing bridge and poker or reading, sleeping, and sweating in our bunks as the soot-spewing train chugged through the deserts or stopped at isolated sidings. Stops were made at towns where boxed meals and drinking water were delivered to us. Five soot-filled, bathless days later we arrived at San Antonio, or more exactly at an isolated marshaling yard where a mile away tall buildings poked into the sky.

The engine left us and we remained motionless for several hours in the sticky Gulf Coast midday. The odors of unwashed bodies increased markedly as the hot and humid day wore on. To add to these discomforts, lightning and thunder in a towering, black thunderhead bore down on us. We climbed back into the cars and gazed forlornly at torrents of rain. In a sudden inspiration I shouted, "LET'S TAKE A SHOWER!" Somebody said to me, "That's the only smart thing I ever heard you say." In a minute, fifty naked cadets were bathing in the rain, hoping it would continue long enough to rinse off the soap.

Refreshed and having been switched to another rail line, we rattled south toward Corpus Christi where we arrived the next day at about noon. There an officer ordered us to get into uniform and board waiting buses. He wore khakis with a short-sleeve shirt and open collar. Dress blues, consisting of a necktie and a heavy woolen suit capable of fending off a blizzard, were all we had, and in them we arrived at Main Station, Corpus Christi, after a long stifling ride through a typical Gulf Coast 95 degrees with matching humidity level.

The greeting ceremony was mercifully brief as we stood at attention in the noonday sun on steaming asphalt outside our assigned barracks. Great blotches of sweat oozed from our backs and armpits. I expected someone to faint from hyperthermia, perhaps me, but it didn't happen. We were dismissed, picked up our seabags, and sought the shade of the barracks to shed our blue uniforms. One large cadet shed his coat and wrung out a pint of sweat.

Blues would not be worn again for months. A sign on the door to the barracks read: WELCOME TO CORPUS CHRISTI THE LARGEST NAVAL AIR TRAINING CENTER IN THE WORLD.

5

Flying Those Turkey Vultee Vibrators

I could see that these barracks were an improvement over Livermore. They looked new and permanent and instead of forty, only six of us slept in one room. I learned that construction had begun on the Main Station, also called Main Side, in mid-1940. It had no more history or naval atmosphere than Livermore, only slightly more than Del Monte, and certainly less than San Francisco; no aura of mossy naval tradition here. If Pensacola cradled naval aviation, Corpus Christi bedded its adult clone. My status in the Navy had improved, an indication that the hallowed principle of "rank hath its privileges" was alive even at our low level.

The Navy had carved Main Side from a treeless, swampy coastal plain fronting on Corpus Christi bay. It had a naked look, since the landscaping plants were still in their infancy. Despite the newness of the buildings, they lacked dignity; they were institutional, not much different from the impermanent facilities at Livermore. They didn't have the look and feel of naval power I had expected, but seemed more like an anonymous civilian administrative facility or light manufacturing center with uniforms and airplanes.

The stifling heat and humidity of September on the Gulf Coast wilted me, and the sun's reflections on the metallic gray bay made me squint and want to loaf in the shade. Cool air could only be found aloft. I missed living in the West, where air is dry and cooling, where mountains shape the horizon and valleys catch their shadows, where prairies roll like ocean swells, where sand warms the feet of sea cliffs and trees turn bent backs to the west wind. But the anticipated pleasure of growing as an aviator and finishing flight training offset the negatives. This place had to be endured while nurturing the certainty that conditions could only improve from here. For now, I would be doing what I wanted to do—flying. I would enjoy the camaraderie of others who shared the same goals and then move on.

We were billeted in transients' barracks, the same that housed cadets who had just finished training, had been commissioned, and would move elsewhere to operational training in combat aircraft. They strutted about, dressing for the first time in their new uniforms with golden wings and bars. I was envious. I wondered if the Navy had brought us together intentionally. If so, it was a clever ploy to give heart and hope to new arrivals, a carrot and stick deal.

I asked one newly commissioned man for any words of wisdom that might help me in the training ahead. He laughed. "Don't take chances and stay out of trouble," he said. I knew that already. I saw nothing special in these men, just cadets in new clothes. If those guys could do it, so could I.

My stay at Main Side was short. Within two days they sent me to Cuddihy Field, an outlying facility, for basic military flight training with cadets I didn't know. I had learned to expect the change of faces.

Cuddihy Field stood barely above surrounding swampy ground a few miles inland from the Main Station. There we were introduced

The Vultee SNV, a two-seat, low-wing monoplane, was detested by all as the "Vultee Vibrator."
U.S. Naval Institute

to flying in "service-type aircraft." That meant aircraft that had controls, an instrument panel, and radios in an enclosed cockpit similar to those in combat aircraft. We would fly the two-seat SNV, a low-wing monoplane built by Vultee and detested by all as the "Vultee Vibrator." I never heard anyone say anything good about it

I flew with an instructor, then solo for a few hours. Formation flying in the Vibrator turned out to be easy. The main hazard was a midair collision that could chop off a tail or wing, requiring you to "hit the silk," short for parachute jump.

But instrument flying strained my mind and emotions. I flew in the rear cockpit of the Vibrator under a canvas hood that shut out all sight of land and sky. The feeling of being part of the world was lost. I no longer felt the exhilaration of seeing all those panoramas, landscapes, clouds, and blue sky. In their stead, I stared into a gloomy cave with many instruments, like the eyes of unfriendly beasts. My survival instincts sharpened, for the hazards were real. During 1943, part of which I trained at Corpus Christi, fifty-nine cadets died in aircraft accidents, casualties of war as certain as if they had fallen in combat.

When flying on instruments, I learned to believe what the instruments indicated and to ignore my body sensations, because they lied. Since I couldn't see the real horizon, I flew an airplane silhouette against a gyro-stabilized artificial horizon with the help of an altimeter, airspeed indicator, directional gyro, engine power gauges, and other instruments. It took only a few hours under the hood to learn to keep them all reading in the correct ranges and to convince myself that I must learn instrument flying exceedingly well to survive.

I roomed with a lanky, laconic cadet from West Texas, predictably nicknamed "Tex." Tex knew what he disliked, instrument flying for one. After a week of flying under the hood he flopped in his bunk and stared at the ceiling. "Tex, are you all right?" Without moving an eye he drawled, "Ah'll die flyin' fuckin' instruments. Send my gear to my mama."

Navigating on a radio range with four narrow radio beams audible on an airplane's radio, I learned, gave rise to the expression "on the beam." I spent what seemed like endless hours under the hood boring holes in the sky to find and stay on a beam. After two ninety-minute flights in one day, I was spent.

Link trainers, in which we simulated radio range flying, were earthbound contraptions that contained the instruments and controls of an airplane. Rows of them, like truncated airplane embryos, stood in a hangarlike room. A crablike device connected to each trainer crawled about on a plotting table marking where you had flown on the radio range. The instructor had a duplicate set of instruments to watch. As a flight training aid, they were of little value, since they neither felt nor sounded like an airplane but they drilled you on radio range procedures. My reactions to them ranged from boredom to frustration. "Tex," I asked, one evening, "how's it going in the Link trainers?"

"Today I done spun that mothah in."

Each Link trainer had a WAVE (a female enlisted person) as an instructor, which gave cadets an opportunity to meet them and perhaps get a date. I got a "down" in the WAVE-dating part of the program, but not from lack of effort. Those young women had talked to and helped train hundreds of cadets who had only one thing on their minds besides flying. They were picky; I was never a pickee.

The town of Corpus Christi had become an instant Navy town in early 1942 when the Navy brought sixty thousand uniformed personnel into the area. By 1943, when I arrived, the original flavor of the place had been drowned by a tsunami of uniformed men and women, uniform tailor shops, and bars. A liberty there wasted time and money; women were scarce and booze expensive. At the local watering holes where women out for a good time showed themselves, cadets didn't have a chance among the dozens of well-heeled officers on the prowl. I felt like a jackal on the fringe of a lion pride. What remained were movies, parks, churches, and window-shopping for bargains in officers' uniforms that I hoped to buy soon. No one escaped from the humdrum of the Texas Coast, because Corpus was the most cosmopolitan city in that part of Texas. It was downhill, one redneck town after another, until you got to San Antonio, some 150 miles away, and that place swarmed with enlisted Army beetle crunchers. The smart cadets stayed on the air station where the facilities were good and the chow free while the rest of us bucked the odds in town.

The most dreaded and trying part of instrument training, "unusual attitude training," came near the end of our stay at Cuddihy. It amounted to a series of flights in which the instructor maneuvered the airplane into an unusual attitude—inverted, dive, stall, steep bank, and so on—from which you had to recover using only the instruments. My instructor flew the airplane through a series of wild stunts that had the feel of a bucking bronco. When the gyro-controlled instruments had tumbled and were unusable, he said, "Cadet, you've got it." I had to ignore the messages my senses were sending me and note the conditions indicated by the instruments to bring the airplane back to straight and level flight. Tex called it, "Bull ridin' blindfolded." In a real-life flight situation you had to make such a recovery or it meant a parachute jump or death in a crash, a grim choice. Sometimes a lucky pilot fell out of the bottom of a cloud with enough altitude to recover visually, like waking from a nightmare.

In mid-November, the long stay at Cuddihy field flying those turkey Vultee Vibrators ended. Once more the cards were shuffled. Tex and I were dealt to an outlying station near Kingsville, thirty-five miles southwest along the coast from Corpus Christi, for advanced training, the final stage before graduating.

6

The End of a Long Beginning

Tex and I and a clutch of other cadets, all grateful to leave Cuddihy, were bused to Kingsville, still on the flat, humid, swampy, treeless plain along the Gulf.

Arbitrary room assignment put me with Tex and three cadets I didn't know: Dick, a blond, confident, graceful athlete from Wisconsin; Boston Boy, a shy naive man with an irritating, whiny New England accent; and Griff from the South, a covert loner, with a weak, moist handshake. Except for Griff, we were in the same training group of six and began a packed schedule of formation flying, gunnery, navigation, instruments, dog fighting, and aerobatics, frequently practicing alone.

We flew the SNJ, a low-wing monoplane with a 500-horsepower engine, controllable pitch propeller, and retractable landing gear, a change from the Vibrator, like swapping a jackass for a mustang. It had most of the characteristics of a fighter plane but less power. The SNJ was aviator-friendly and safe. Fun flying had returned after all those dreary hours under the instrument hood.

We became a closely knit team, flying, learning, and playing together. No matter how tired from the previous night's liberty, rain or shine, Dick was up, prodding us to life, making us keep the

The North American SNJ "Texan" advance trainer was a low-wing monoplane with a 500-horsepower engine, controllable pitch propeller, and retractable landing gear. The change from the "Vultee Vibrator" was like swapping a jackass for a mustang.
U.S. Naval Institute

schedule, chanting the flight hours we needed to finish, "only forty more hours, forty more hours." Such was our determination in our push to finish, we stood by in bad weather, hoping to be the first in the air when the sky cleared.

Pulling the SNJ's wheels up, as a bird tucks in its legs, made me feel that I had quit the earth to become a creature of the air, challenged by towering white clouds; mountains drifting in the sky invited me to explore their fluffy canyons, tunnels, cliffs, holes, and overhangs of infinite variety. The exhilarating sense of speed when near them was a gift of nature given only to aviators and birds.

But all was not exhilarating on one flight when I led a group of three. Dinging around among the clouds, I lost track of our location as the cloud cover increased. I soon had only glimpses of the ground.

An empty feeling stirred my gut. I had to get below the clouds to find my location and avoid a blind descent on instruments, but I feared diving through a hole since I might run into unseen aircraft. The cloud openings grew smaller, widening the void in my gut that prodded me relentlessly. I had to dive through one of them and hope for the best. I chopped back the throttle and started down. In a few seconds I realized that was a bad move because now the two planes on my wings overran me and had to zigzag and fishtail to get back into formation. I knew they were pissed by the way they had to jerk their planes around. The dive was awkward but we leveled out just below the clouds at 500 feet. With the luck that preserves the inept innocent, I flew straight at a distinctive road intersection we all recognized, the only such landmark within ten miles. My gut felt better but my poor leadership saddened me. Back on the ground, I endured a chewing out by Dick and Tex, who had been flying with me. I took it passively for I knew they were right. I vowed never again to blunder into such a threatening, avoidable situation.

Flights over the Gulf gave me my first feel for the vast emptiness of the sea and sky that stretched away to infinity. On hazy days the two almost merged, conspiratorially erasing the horizon, leaving me straining for something on which to focus. Nothing on the water or in the air looked friendly. I sensed that I had invaded a private realm. Sea and sky waited patiently for me to make a mistake, and if I did, they would watch impassively. I had to depend on myself. I wouldn't be able to walk away from a water landing. During navigational flights over land, I knew I had a security blanket, a safety net. The ground would catch me no matter how I came down, and with luck, I could walk away from a landing.

Inland from Kingsville, gray green mesquite blanketed the coastal plain that stretched to the horizon with only occasional dirt roads and patchy oil installations scratched from the mesquite. Navigating there was almost as uncertain as over the Gulf. I had to make a routine training flight inland to a small town, turn left, fly to another, and return to Kingsville. I flew on a magnetic heading at low altitude across the sea of mesquite; the only moving thing was the shadow of my plane, like a dog on a leash. I felt lonely and insecure. After an interval of time, roofs shone in the distance. I headed for them and circled; the right name was painted on a roof, nearly awash in vegetation. I wondered why anyone would choose to live there. I turned on course to the second town, found it barely afloat in mesquite, and headed toward what I thought of as home. Before long the Gulf sparkled in the distance. All was well again. There sat Kingsville and the station a few miles away. A friendly woman's voice cleared me for landing. I slipped into the traffic pattern, dropped my landing gear, and touched down. Home again.

Until I came to Kingsville, training had concentrated on flying the airplanes safely, but here we learned to use them as weapons. The SNJ mounted a machine gun for firing on a cloth sleeve, towed by one of our team, on which our paint-tipped bullets would leave marks. The rest of us followed the tow plane out to sea where the gunnery runs started above and abeam of the tow plane. We peeled off one at a time, stooped in a smooth S-turn to bring the sleeve into our gunsight, fired a short burst, swept under the sleeve, and zoomed up to the opposite side of the tow plane for another run. Only soaring birds can match the smooth flow and grace of a gunnery run.

One week, Griff got the idea of escaping the deadening environment of Kingsville by going to Mexico for a weekend liberty. But how to get there? He then astounded us by announcing, "We can all ride down in my car." Cadets were forbidden to have automobiles, but Griff apparently didn't believe that rule applied to him. He didn't explain why his car was there, nor did we question him for fear he might withdraw his offer.

We were skeptical of his promise, but on Saturday morning Dick, Tex, Boston Boy, and I followed him through the station gate to his car, a two-door sedan of recent vintage, in, of all places, the officers' parking lot. We were mystified but that didn't stop us from heading toward Mexico. Gasoline was tightly rationed then.

I wondered where in hell he got the gasoline and where in hell he got the .45-caliber automatic pistol he waved around and then returned to a holster hidden behind the dashboard. In the back-seat Tex's raised eyebrows plainly asked, "What's with this guy?" All the signs of trouble were plain for me to see, but I just drifted along with the group.

Griff drove to the border town of McAllen where we rented a couple of rooms at a motel. We then crossed the Rio Grande to Reynosa, a grubby, mean-looking Mexican town with dusty streets, buildings, and people. The locals had booze, gasoline, sex, and other items for sale to gringos, items that were in short supply in Texas. Being among the few gringos there that Saturday, we became very popular. Toward evening, the owner of a cantina enticed us in with boasts of excellent food, drink, and women. While we sat drinking moderately and playing coy with the senoritas, Boston Boy disappeared in the direction of the men's room. When he didn't return soon, I checked and found he wasn't there. We began asking questions but received only evasive answers from the ladies and the bartender. Dick finally demanded an answer from the bartender who shouted something; a woman answered and hurried into a back room. In a few minutes, Boston Boy reappeared slouching drunkenly with a silly grin on his face, his uniform wrinkled, and his tie askew. "Where in hell have you been?" Dick demanded.

"I've been screwing a senorita. That's why we came here wasn't it?"

Tex asked, "Did y'all use a condom?"

"I didn't have a damn condom."

"Yuh stupid Yankee. Y'all probably got a dose of clap or worse."

Dick stood up abruptly and put on his hat, "We've got to go back to McAllen and get you a VD prophylaxis or you'll be in the clap shack and be washed out." Griff bought a couple of quarts of Waterfill and Fraser whiskey, hid them under the seat of the car, and returned to McAllen where Boston Boy underwent the indignity of an anti-VD treatment.

The next morning we checked out of the motel, drove a mile out of town, and stashed our smuggled whiskey near a billboard, then drove back to Reynosa, did a little shopping, purchased two more quarts of Waterfill and Fraser's finest whiskey, and headed for Kingsville. At the U.S. Customs station at the McAllen end of the Rio Grande River bridge, we tried to look casual and innocent, which was probably a mistake. The customs officer said, "Everyone out of the car." In less than a minute he found the whiskey. It became increasingly clear that I had used poor judgment in agreeing to make this trip.

There ensued a prolonged, painful, embarrassing period of filling out smuggling citations. The whiskey, of course, was confiscated. Fines were assessed and paid. Griff, a pale ghost, wandered about nervously, probably thinking about the gun the inspector had not discovered. The customs officer recorded the name and address of our naval unit and sent shocks though our ranks by saying, "A report will be forwarded to your commanding officer." I could only think of the worst consequences the Navy could inflict upon me: wash me out of the program and give me a one-way ticket to Great Lakes. The offense stated on the citations, "petty smuggling," seemed mild compared to what it would have been if they had found the gun. We were a melancholy, contemplative bunch of cadets who left McAllen. Not too distracted, however, to forget the whiskey stashed by the billboard. That eased the pain somewhat, and our spirits revived. Griff sold it to an enlisted man we met on the street in Kingsville.

For several days, we expected the ax to fall from the commanding officer. After a week, we began to relax. Apparently no report of our stupidity ever came to the air station. It surprised me that all of us had agreed to go to Mexico in Griff's car since his having it in the first place should have been warning enough that he was a scofflaw or worse. Two weeks later, when I returned to our room, Dick fumed, "Griff stole my watch. I'd kill the son of a bitch, but he's gone, moved out with all his gear." This strange event began to clarify when my three roommates and I were excused from all scheduled activities and ordered to report to the administration building.

At the appointed time and place, we found waiting in a hallway a dozen gloomy cadets we didn't know from Main Side and Cabaniss Field, a basic training field like Cuddihy. They hinted that this gathering had something to do with Griff. Griff arrived looking pale and worried. He glanced around and seemed to recognize everyone. He made weak attempts to chat but was shunned. Dick seethed at the sight of him. An officer opened a door nearby and called us to come in one at a time. Before I was invited into the room, I had concluded we were about to face some kind of a hearing. It was, in fact, a court of inquiry. Several stern-faced officers sat at a table facing an empty chair. A stenographer sat, with pen poised. I took an oath of truthfulness and an officer waved to the empty chair still faintly warm and sweaty from the preceding cadet. One officer, no doubt an attorney, shuffled through some papers, whispered to the men at the table, turned toward me, fixed me with hard eyes, and began. "Cadet, state your full name." That was easy. The questions that followed were harder. He established that I had shared a room with Griff for several weeks and went on to ask about Griff's car. Had I ridden in it? How often and where? I feared that whatever Griff had done might somehow implicate me and jeopardize my place in the training program. I could feel sweat trickling from my armpits.

The truthful answers that I gave sounded like nails being pounded into Griff's coffin. The officer wrung it all out of me and sent me out an escape door to dry. I felt vaguely guilty about being a snitch and helping the other side, the authorities. But that wore off after talking to my roommates. We agreed that it didn't seem likely that all of us would be guilty and punished by our association with Griff. But the fear of failure always lurked in the back of my mind. No more half-baked expeditions for me; I had too much at stake.

I never heard anything official about the inquiry, but we found out enough to know that the main charge against Griff was theft of another cadet's money in an unbelievably audacious and ill-timed caper. We pieced together most of the scenario of his scam. Payday came once a month. A paymaster paid in cash. Cadet units were scheduled to be paid at different times of the day. We filled out a cash-withdrawal form and stood in line leading to the paymaster's desk. He took the form, had us sign a receipt, recorded the payment in our pay record, and counted the cash into our hands. One such payday, a cadet presented his cash-withdrawal form only to have the paymaster ask him why he was in the line again, since he had just withdrawn all the pay he had coming. The astonished cadet protested vehemently that this was his first time in line. The paymaster remembered the cadet who had just made the withdrawal and had him stopped before he left the building. It was Griff.

I guessed that Griff had used this scheme at other times and places, but this time he had had the bad luck of stealing from a cadet who stood close behind him in line, too close for him to sneak away. How he selected a cadet to steal from and forged the signature and any identification documents he needed wasn't known. None of us ever heard anything about Griff again. He'd been an unnecessary, irritating distraction to us and now seemed to have disappeared from the face of the earth. And good riddance.

Dick organized all his activities, from brushing his teeth to his sex life, to the point of being amusing. As Christmas approached, he produced his Christmas card list and showed it to me. Some of the names were crossed out or had little checks next to them. I asked him about that. "Those crossed out are people I sent cards to last year, but they didn't send me one. Those with a check sent cards, and so they will get one from me this year." There were some additions to the list, including me, that were about to receive their first card from him. Since I didn't send cards, my name would be crossed out soon. He recorded some of his less benign activities in much the same way.

As at Cuddihy field, Kingsville had a "squadron" of Link trainers, complete with enlisted WAVE operators. Dick's good looks and charm caused one of them to choose him as a sex partner. On weekend liberty, they met in Corpus Christi and spent most of their time in a hotel room. Dick had a reference book entitled *The 54 Best Positions for Coitus, Illustrated*. Like his Christmas list, the book had checks and cross-outs by each position. He also applied grades A, B, C, and so on to W for withdrew and I for incomplete. His graphic descriptions made it easy to visualize him in a snarl of limbs making checkmarks or cross-outs in the book as each position was attempted and evaluated. He marked the book where he stopped so he could begin again the next weekend, perhaps with a few review exercises. I tried not to let my envy show when he described these exploits.

The way he talked about sex seemed as coolly dispassionate as a scientific experiment. Although we laughed at the accounts of his exploits, for me it was nervous laughter, like one hears following a tasteless joke. He never expressed any affection for the woman. It was just a self-satisfying physical exercise devoid of any emotional content. It seemed too detached for a relationship that most of us felt should have elements of mutual caring, seduction, reluctant yielding, and passionate release, followed by misgivings, regrets, and a heap of guilt. He had opened a new window for me on sex as a purely physical gratification akin to masturbation. But all such thoughts were just sour grapes.

Dick had a hometown sweetheart whom he intended to marry some day. In her pictures, she looked wholesome, conservatively groomed and primly dressed, obviously a "nice" girl, hands folded in her lap, knees together, and ankles crossed. He planned to invite her to visit after he graduated. Until then he said, "What better activity is there for entertainment and preparation for marriage?" It struck me that he had organized a future that, realistically, defied organizing.

Toward the end of the flight syllabus at Kingsville was the inevitable night flying, some as single plane flights and others in formations of two or three planes. It was no easier in the SNJ than in any of the other planes. On a dark night, the running lights of the other planes in the formation had a near-hypnotic effect that I had to struggle against. I began to see tiny spots of light in groups that approached and passed rapidly in random directions, like shiny beads cascading on black velvet. Was I seeing things that weren't there?

After landing, I asked the other pilots if they had seen anything that resembled what I had. They had seen the lights and were as puzzled as I. It comforted me to know I was not alone in this. We finally concluded that they were reflections of our running lights from the eyes of flocks of migratory waterfowl. That experience did nothing to make me enthusiastic about night flying.

The SNJ was the first plane with retractable wheels any of us had flown. As a safety device to avoid a wheels-up landing, a horn mounted behind the pilot's head would sound when the wheels were retracted and the throttle lever moved to the idle position. According to an oft-repeated story, the control tower saw an SNJ that had been cleared to land coming in with its wheels up and transmitted an urgent message to the pilot to put his wheels down. When the wheels did not come down they commanded him not to land. The plane landed anyway wheels-up. When the pilot was asked why he didn't follow the tower's instructions he answered, "I couldn't understand the tower because a damn loud horn was sounding in the cockpit."

In early February 1944, the seemingly endless cadet flight training wound down, my last flight an anticlimax. I don't remember it, except for being on the ground in the twilight, affectionately patting the plane as I would a faithful dog. Overhead, planes droned in the traffic pattern, landed, and taxied in as they had for months. For me, cadet flying had ended, a goal attained, an unknown future opened. No congratulations were offered, no celebrations planned or improvised. I met Dick in our room. "Let's play some table tennis," he said.

"Yeah, let's play."

I had become a competent aviator, having logged 350 hours, ready to fly the newest carrier aircraft. The ultimate test would be to fly from aircraft carriers into combat. Before I prepared for that, I would be commissioned and designated a naval aviator, seventeen months after my first training flight in a Piper Cub in Susanville. Many of my schoolmates had long since gone to islands in the Pacific, Europe, or North Africa, from where some would never return. Meanwhile, I had continued training with no end in sight.

Occasionally, the military offers career options. We were offered the choice of a commission in the Navy or the Marine Corps, an easy decision for me. I had joined the Navy and there I wanted to stay. I could think of no reason to join what seemed like a subsidiary activity to the main event. Besides, Marines' uniforms were too flashy for my tastes.

A few days later Dick, Tex, Boston Boy, and I packed our gear and took a bus to Main Side. We were hauled to the same transients' barracks we had stayed in when we had arrived six months earlier. Tex and Boston Boy drifted away, lost to me in the twisting currents of war. In the next room I discovered my friend from Livermore, Smoggy Paul. Dick and I joined forces with him for this final push to escape cadetdom.

The first step took us into uniform shops in Corpus Christi where smooth-talking salesmen persuaded us to buy their tailor-made uniforms that were, in fact, probably sewed together by women in sweatshops in New York. Though the uniforms did not fit well, we loved them when accented by golden bars, wings, and braid. We were now the envy of cadets arriving from primary training stations. We strutted shamelessly in their presence.

While we waited at Main Side, they scheduled us for a secret briefing. We took a bus to a small frame building a mile away surrounded by high chain-link fence. On the roof, several antennas rotated. We had to present identification and authorization papers to be admitted, then were escorted to a small auditorium. There we received a lecture on the need for absolute secrecy about what we were about to see. Obviously something important was taking place here. We were shown a movie of a dive-bomber equipped with a system called radar (*ra*dio, *d*etecting *a*nd *r*anging), the first time we had heard that word. Radar could search large areas for enemy ships and aircraft in all weather conditions.

Several operating systems were in the building. On the radar scopes we could see bright moving blips that were airplanes landing and taking off from Main Side. I was deeply impressed and pleased to be let in on such an important secret. None of us had the faintest idea of how it worked. They admonished us that the existence of this system must not be discussed outside of that building. I had received and enjoyed the first touch of ever-increasing responsibility that is an officer's lot.

We waited for a stack of paperwork to be prepared, an impersonal, mechanical procedure that involved much standing in line waiting for yeomen to complete the administrative details. We had suffered, been tested, and knew we were something special, but to them we were just more fresh-faced, anonymous cadets like the hundreds they had seen last month, the month before that, and the year before that. I wouldn't escape the cadet feeling and image until I left this aviator factory.

Dressed as an officer, I felt reborn. The shine on my buttons, braid, wings, and bars announced to everyone that here was a green ensign, but that was better than being in the limbo world of cadets. The first time an enlisted man saluted me, he was gone before I realized what had happened.

We mustered for a picture with all others commissioned that week, the only event that even faintly resembled a graduation ceremony, saluted only by a camera click. The real graduation would be when I was out of the gate headed to my next station. It would be the end of a long beginning.

We were asked to state our preferences for the type of aircraft we wanted to fly in combat. My first choice was fighters, because I thought my aptitude for that kind of flying equal to any cadet I had met in the program, and my "loner" instincts surfaced. I didn't want to be responsible for an aircrewman riding in the backseat. They gave me my second choice, dive-bombers, which came with an aircrewman.

The cards were shuffled again. Dick and I were sent to Cecil Field near Jacksonville, Florida, for dive-bomber training. Paul would also fly dive-bombers but train at a field in southern Florida. We had four days to get there, and rail was the best means of transport. Dick made a quick trip home to see his family and sweetheart.

Civilians packed our train to Florida forcing Paul and me, along with a couple of others, to stand outside the toilet at one end of a car. A long tiring ride lay ahead of us to New Orleans, eighteen hours away. The train made many stops; people got on but few got off. No seat vacancies appeared. As the night wore on, we were forced to sit on the floor leaning against our luggage, quite undignified for a couple of proud naval officers in new uniforms. Rank got us no privileges in that situation.

We struck up a conversation with another standee, now a sitee also, a redneck from Louisiana. He'd been taking nips from a pint bottle and was holding up well. He finally asked Paul and me, "Ah got some applejack, y'all want a swig?"

I didn't know about applejack. I thought it a quaint way of saying cider. I took a mouthful before I realized it was nothing like apple cider but more like high-proof whiskey. It might even have been moonshine. My reaction seemed to amuse him. With tears in my eyes, fire in my throat, fumes in my sinuses, and a suppressed cough in my lungs, I soon had applejack in my stomach. When Paul took his nip, his eyes bulged and he stopped breathing until he forced it down. Despite our temporary discomfort, our friend with the applejack had helped ease the pain of the ride.

Early the next afternoon, in New Orleans, we left the train and took a hotel room to shower and rest. That evening, we waited in line to eat at the hotel restaurant. A short distance ahead of us stood two young women dressed, groomed, and coifed for a night out. We eyed them hungrily. Within a few minutes, they had given up their places in line and were now just ahead of us. Our golden naval aviator magic had captivated them. They would be the first of many dominoes to fall on their backs before us. One of the women turned to us, flashed a charming smile, and said, "If y'all share a table with us we'll get seated sooner." I felt a little ashamed. This would be just too easy. That y'all stuff intoxicated me. I winked at Paul and said, "Good idea."

They must have known that we were recently released from the monastic austerity of cadet social life on the Texas coast. Near the end of the meal, the waiter asked if we would like an after-dinner drink. The women thought for a minute and said, "A demitasse, please." Paul and I exchanged blank glances. It sounded so sophisticated and refined I recklessly said, "We'll have the same." Hell, it was just an expensive skinny cup of strong coffee. After we'd paid the check, the women became restive, remembered they had an engagement elsewhere, gave us a sugary "good-bye y'all," and departed. As their slinky backsides disappeared, Paul nudged me, "Y'all are one smooth operator."

The next day, two wiser cadets dressed as officers rolled easterly along the Gulf Coast on a rail line above swamps, then through the piney woods of northern Florida. At Jacksonville we parted. Paul continued south and I caught a Navy bus to nearby Cecil Field. I never saw Paul again.

It was now early March 1944. U.S. forces in the Pacific had captured the Marshall Islands and were poised to attack the Marianas. Our submarines had decimated the Japanese merchant marine, choking down their war-making potential. In Europe, the Soviets were pushing the Germans out of Russia. The Allies had captured Rome and were preparing for a cross-channel invasion of Western Europe.

The thrill of flying the same combat aircraft that had stopped the Japanese at Midway lay just ahead.

7

Dive-Bombing at Cecil Field

Cecil Field occupied a fenced clearing chopped out of deserted piney woods ten miles from Jacksonville. Some trees had been left standing between the buildings, all cast from the same molds that made the buildings at other stations. The landing area, tarmac, and hangars were nothing new, in short just another standard training facility, but a pleasant setting compared to the swamps around the airfields at Corpus Christi. Only the airplanes were different, rows of squat SBD dive-bombers. The sole function of Cecil Field was to teach pilots to fly them for the purposes for which they had been built, dive bombing and landing on aircraft carriers.

Each room in the BOQ slept three men, a clear sign that my status had changed for the better. I liked the additional privacy. Dick, my buddy from Kingsville and the only one of the ten in our training group I knew, bunked with two strangers down the hall. My two new roommates, Sam and Vic, were congenial southerners I learned to enjoy and respect. They were exceptionally handsome, fun-loving men. Their soft, southern accents and gentle manners were infectious to the point that I soon discovered that my speech and actions began to echo theirs. We began a long-lasting three-cornered friendship.

Adjusting to my hard-won status as an officer was an exhilarating experience. Enlisted men addressed me as "sir" and saluted. I left the station without a pass, ate at the officers' mess, drank in the club, and listened to battle-hardened aviators talk about Guadalcanal, Rabaul, Midway, and the Philippines. I was awed by them and wondered how I would measure up in combat. Time would tell.

So began another flight training stint. The SBD was the first plane I had flown that lacked dual controls. I had only a familiarization lecture and a cockpit checkout then was told to take her up, rather like taking the family car for a spin around the block for the first time. Most flights were dive-bombing and field carrier landing practice, skills that would make us effective in the fleet. The first could hurt the enemy; the second could preserve our skins by getting us back aboard a carrier.

Our training officer, Lieutenant Crawford, a combat veteran, lived off the station with his wife. We saw him only when he was doing his job as our instructor and adviser. In seven weeks, one hundred flying hours, he would make carrier-ready dive-bomber pilots out of us. His pleasing tidewater Virginia accent carried authority when he said, "We'll go oot now, take off and join up at a-boot two thousand feet." He knew his job, did it well, and turned out to be a smooth, predictable aviator. I felt secure flying on his wing.

Crawford was modest and reserved. In our first meeting he told us frankly, "Dive-bombing is a dangerous operation, but you can reduce the hazards by thinking ahead and executing each dive according to plan, no fancy maneuvers or improvising until you are more experienced." While hardening his voice, he continued, "High-octane gasoline is in short supply, so we use gasoline of lower octane, not recommended for the SBD. It fouls the spark plugs and causes irregular running when the engine is cold. Be certain that the engine is at operating temperature and test the magnetos at maximum power before taking off."

Vic asked, "Has this low-octane gasoline caused any accidents?"

"Yes, several, but never if the engine was properly warmed up. If the RPM at full power drops more than 400 rpms on one mag, or you hear any 'popping,' don't take off until the engine smooths out."

Vic looked at me and raised his eyebrows, a silent "Ye gods, flying is dangerous enough without using punk gasoline."

The SBDs, built by Douglas Aircraft Company, had been in service since before the war and had been thoroughly tested in combat. Some of the planes at Cecil Field had been around for a long time. Some had seen combat. All showed their age. They were not the fighter aircraft I had hoped to fly, but they had a sturdy look about them, like a tugboat, that appealed to my feelings of self-preservation. Still, they were not the powerful, pugnacious-looking Hellcats or the sleek, graceful inverted gull-wing Corsair fighters.

Crawford's warning about low-octane gasoline proved not to be enough. I took off one morning followed by Sam. As I climbed into the traffic pattern I looked back to watch Sam, one hundred feet above the end of the runway suddenly begin a shallow glide

Dive-bombing training group, Cecil Field, Jacksonville, Florida, in front of a Douglas SBD "Dauntless" dive-bomber. Ensign Vernon is standing second from right.

toward the trees, which soon began to fall like wheat under a sickle. He careened to a stop. His aircrewman jumped out and put distance between himself and the plane. Sam sat in the plane, his left elbow on the edge of the cockpit and his cheek resting on his fist. I called MAYDAY several times into my microphone but got no answer. I was not transmitting except on the intercom. By the time I had figured that out, several emergency vehicles were already speeding, lights flashing, toward the end of the runway nearest Sam's plane. Fortunately no fire started. Sam was OK. He spent the rest of the day at the medical dispensary for checkups.

It was the first crash I had seen. It amazed me that the plane was so strong that it knocked down all those trees and Sam didn't receive a scratch. The realization that I had witnessed the near death of a friend jolted me back to the reality of the hazards of military flying.

That evening, Vic and I were in our room quietly discussing how the crash might affect Sam's standing in the Navy, when he appeared at the door looking pale. He held up his hand and said, "Don't ask. The fuckin' engine in that old clunker just quit cold."

"OK, OK, roomie," Vic said, "Let's have a drink at the club to celebrate your triumphant return. You're the envy of our group 'cuz you need to down only four more planes to become an ace." We were certain the accident resulted from the low-octane gasoline, but as usual, the station command covered its behind by charging it to "pilot error" for not properly testing the engine before takeoff.

When practicing dive-bombing, we dropped miniature, cast-steel bombs, about the size of a beer bottle, which had the same fall trajectory as large bombs. An explosive charge resembling a shotgun shell loaded in the bombs released a puff of white smoke at the point of impact. The bombs were carried in a rack under the wing. A selected bomb released when we pressed a button called the "pickle" on top of the control stick. In the jargon of dive-bombers, you would "pickle it off." We aimed at a bull's-eye

marked with white lines in a clearing where an observer recorded
and announced to the pilot the location of each of his drops, such
as, two hundred feet at three o'clock.

We dive-bombed in groups of four or more planes. As we
neared the target at 15,000 feet, we were in a strung-out echelon like
a gaggle of wild geese. We nosed down into a high-speed approach
toward the peel-off point at 12,000 feet, positioned nearly vertically
above the target. During the high-speed approach, you had to see
the target more than four miles away to anticipate the peel-off
maneuver required to get lined up on the target. A peel-off consisted of a sharp, steep pull-up and wingover to nearly inverted
flight. You had to tip your head far back to keep the target in sight,
then pull the nose down toward it and open the dive brakes. To dive
nearly vertically at high speed and watch the target grow rapidly
in the bombsight was alien to my survival instincts. During a dive,
the pilot's weight rested on the shoulder harness. The plane buf-
feted as you steered it into the dive and onto the target, and speed
increased. You had to aim somewhere in the twelve o'clock position, because the bomb's trajectory would be below the line of
sight. Meanwhile, the altimeter needle spun like a top from 12,000
toward 4,000 feet, and the airspeed indicator left 250 knots headed
for 300 and beyond. The rapid increase of air pressure caused your
ears and sinuses to pop. Flight characteristics of the plane changed
with increased speed. You had to fight the stick and kick the rudders
to hold the plane on the target. Forward pressure on the stick
caused weightlessness and negative g's that pushed you away from
the controls and lifted trash such as cigarette butts and candy wrap-
pers from the bilge, which floated around your head, instruments,
and bombsight. You released the bomb at 3,000 feet and began
pulling out to level flight at 1,500 feet.

The greatest strain was during pullout from the dive when g
forces jammed you into your seat and pulled blood from your brain,
sometimes causing a grayout or a blackout. A grayout was signaled
by a decrease in light intensity and narrowing of your field of

vision, known as the telescope or tunnel effect. Unless the g's were reduced, blackout would follow. Some pilots suffered pain in their sinuses and ears when the rapid change of air pressure was not equalized in them. Occasionally, a ruptured eardrum resulted. But pain usually preceded a rupture in enough time to abort the dive.

Anecdotes about dive-bombing that describe how the dive-bomber did not pull out and hit the ground at twelve o'clock or on the bull's-eye were numerous. The causes of these accidents usually could not be determined, but it is certain that some were caused by the pilot's trying too hard to get lined up with the target and forgetting to check his altitude, or the pilot's simply blacking out. In such an accident, the pilot was scraped up in a basket and sent to his next of kin in a sealed coffin, commonly ballasted with metal or rocks.

I learned after the war that during 1944 one dive-bomber pilot was killed each day in Florida. We read about such accidents with considerable interest, in the hope of learning something that would make it safer. Occasionally, I read the name of a pilot I had known as a cadet. I found my friend Paul's name on one report. Only a few weeks earlier we had been commissioned and traveled to Florida together. It was hard to imagine that anything like that could happen to me. It would always be the other guy.

Perhaps an even more hazardous part of the training was field carrier landing practice. An area the size of an aircraft carrier's deck was outlined on the runway, and a landing signal officer, called the LSO, took his station on the corner of it. We flew in a racetrack pattern, landing with the help of signals from the LSO, who waved brightly colored paddles about the size of a tennis racquet.

The tricky part of this operation was to fly slowly at an altitude of 150 feet in the landing pattern (some trees were more than 50 feet high). Flying low and slow a few knots above stalling speed in a heavy aircraft is akin to walking a high wire without a safety net. On the downwind leg you went through the checkoff list, wheels and flaps down, mixture rich, propeller in low pitch, hatch open and locked, shoulder harness locked, and so on. When you could see the LSO abeam to port, you began losing altitude in a turn of 180 degrees that would put you in landing position at an altitude of about 20 feet, with the LSO abeam. During the turn, the LSO signaled you to adjust your turn, altitude, and speed to get into the "groove." If you approached OK you would get a "cut" signal, the LSO cutting his throat with his right signal paddle. You cut the power, stalled the airplane, thumped to the runway, and then took off for another try. If you approached too high, too fast, or "sucked flat in the groove," you would receive a wave-off, both paddles waved back and forth over his head, like some calisthenic exercises. You applied full power and went around for another try.

Another person entered my life at Cecil Field, an enlisted aircrewman who would ride in the backseat and operate the radio and twin .30-caliber machine guns. His just being there made me uncomfortable, since he was completely dependent on me. He had no controls and would not know how to use them if he did. I felt responsible not only for him but also to his family, a responsibility I hadn't sought and didn't want. He flew on most flights with me and occasionally would be able to fire his guns at a towed sleeve.

Until I came to Cecil Field, I had been conditioned by experience to feel that the men like Bud, Pud, Tex, and Paul who had become my friends were temporary. In the next phase of training others took their places. Now I began to feel that I shared a future with these men. I think others had a similar feeling. We were being funneled down toward common destinations and experiences that would dwarf anything that had gone before in our lives. I felt ready, even eager, to meet them.

Day by day, my bonds with Sam and Vic became stronger. We flew the same airplanes, drank and partied together. The dangers involved seemed to draw us closer, a feeling noted by many who have written about war experiences. In the late afternoon, returning from flights, our flight suits and helmets streaked and saggy from sweat and smelling of hydraulic oil, our life vests and parachute harnesses dangling, we stripped to our street clothes and wandered over to the club for a drink and dinner. Others formed similar alliances. We were all groping for some stable relationships with which we could go forward into the unknown.

For years I had been saddened that Mother, long separated from Dad, had had to support herself working in hotels or people's homes. My newly gained status as an officer gave me an income that exceeded my needs. I could now help her live a better life. I claimed her as a dependent, since she was no longer Dad's dependent. I gave her a monthly allotment of seventy-five dollars from my pay, which the Navy matched under their dependents' policy. She then had an income adequate for her to quit work and fulfill her lifelong desire to go to college. She somehow resurrected her credentials from high school, class of 1909, and matriculated at San Francisco State College, to begin in the summer of 1944, at age fifty-three. That allotment changed her life for the better. College brought joy to her. She earned a B.A. in education and a teacher's credential, followed by a satisfying teaching career that continued into her late seventies.

In May, before she began school, Mother announced that she and my sister Rosemary were planning to visit me, despite the crowded conditions on the railroads. I'm certain that both were anxious for my safety, for they knew aviation was dangerous. My family never spoke of what I know they feared: that I might be killed. Their train would arrive in Jacksonville about noon, an inconvenient time for me to meet them.

Needing to send them a telegram with instructions about my meeting them and finding a place for them to stay, I found the Western Union telegraph office, composed a message, and gave it to a good-looking, smiling young woman at the counter. She scanned it briefly then looked up at me and said, "If we cut a few words, it will save you some money." She laid the form between us on the counter and we leaned over it, so close I could smell her perfume and feel the heat she emanated. My thoughts drifted away from the telegram. She dragged my attention back by pointing out several words that could be deleted. Without thinking about them, I agreed they were not needed. I seemed to have lost my will to resist. "Where have you arranged for them to stay?" she asked. I mumbled that I hadn't made any arrangements. "It's off-season, you know; there are cottages for rent at Jacksonville Beach."

I realized that she had a good idea, and it began to creep into my consciousness that she was interested in me. I looked at her more closely. She was my height, slender, with shoulder-length brown hair framing a harmonious combination of high cheekbones, dark expressive eyes, smooth skin, ample nose, and a friendly smile that showed even white teeth. She moved gracefully, and when she turned, her hair and skirt flared, revealing a graceful neck and athletic legs. That stirred me further. "That's a great idea! How can I contact them?"

She must have decided from the content of my telegram that only a nice boy (not far off the mark) would be entertaining his mother and sister in Jacksonville. "Since they'll arrive during my lunch break, I could meet them at the station," she said. "It's only a block away." She waved aside my objection that it would be too much trouble for her. "No trouble at all. Your mother's name is on your telegram. I'll be able to find them easily." I thanked her and told her I hoped I would see her again soon. Hoped! The understatement of the decade. She was the first friendly, attractive woman I had met in a year.

True to her word, she met them at the train and steered them to a rental agency from which they rented a beach cottage for a couple of weeks. The day they arrived, they called to tell me where they were and how to get there. They waited for me on a porch facing the ocean. When I saw them, I couldn't help running to them for joyous hugging and kissing. They had a nice surprise for me. Mother said, "We brought a friend with us." I looked over her shoulder. There

Laura, my friend from the telegraph office, stood shyly in the door.

That cottage turned out to be a convenient place for Sam, Vic, Laura, and me to spend evenings and days-off taking in the sea, sand, sun, and spirits.

Laura and I became close friends. The velvety, humid sea air seemed to have magnetized us. As my duty at Jacksonville neared its end, we lay on the beach below the sea wall touching, kissing, and caressing innocently. She whispered, "Jim."

"Yes, Laura."

"I wish you didn't have to leave."

"Me too."

"I hate the Navy."

"It's the damn war. Let's go for a swim and forget about it."

Life was good for the moment, but my stay at Jacksonville ended. I had lunch with Laura just before I boarded a train. We nibbled quietly. I couldn't find fitting words but managed to say, "Laura, I'll be gone a long time, probably to the Western Pacific. Will you write?"

"Yes, I'll miss you very much. If we only had more time." Tears shimmered in her eyes. "I'd better go," she whispered. "Good-bye. Please don't kiss me, it will only add to the pain." She got up from the table, patted me on the cheek, and slipped out of the restaurant. Without turning, she raised her arm, waved farewell, and disappeared into a crowd. We had sensed we might never see each other again. It had been a tender interlude. We were hungry, searching young people who had snatched a moment of peace and pleasure in an eddy of the raging river of war. We exchanged a few letters, then nothing. A year later she contacted my mother. She had married an aviator.

My next duty station would be temporary duty at Naval Air Station, Glenview, Illinois, for qualification landings aboard an aircraft carrier. That usually took about five days, after which I would receive fifteen days' leave before reporting to Norfolk for assignment to a squadron.

I planned to visit Dad in Idaho while on leave. Knowing that was scheduled, Mother and Rosemary decided to return to California by way of Dad's home in Wallace, Idaho, where we could have a reunion of our fractured family.

The Chicago train station swirled with servicemen toting duffel bags or trying to sleep on the benches. Forlorn, tired, and frightened country girls, pregnant or with babies, milled about or camped on the floor or benches. This sad flotsam of war funneled through train and bus stations everywhere. I found a Navy bus to ride north to Glenview. I took a seat next to a naval aviation cadet. "What takes you to Glenview?" I asked.

His faraway, hangdog look drifted out the window, "I'm not going to Glenview. I washed out of primary flight training. This bus also goes to Great Lakes Naval Training Station. They'll make a seaman out of me."

"Oh, I'm sorry to hear that. It's not the end of the world, you know. Flight training is long, difficult, and dangerous. You'll feel a lot less strain by being out of it."

"I know all that, but the saddest part is disappointing my family and friends. It will be hard to face them." He fidgeted and stared silently out at the rambling suburbs and then the newly greened Illinois farmland.

The ride had pushed to the back of my mind the reason for going to Glenview until, as we drove through the station, I could see the carrier aircraft on the tarmac. Dowdy, tired-looking SBDs stood in rows. In one of them I would make my first landing aboard a ship. Was I ready for this? Had my training been adequate? Could I pass this test?

When I left the bus I shook the cadet's hand and said, "Good luck."

I could see tears.

"Thanks, you'll need it more than I will," he mumbled.

8

Carrier Qualification
on Lake Michigan

Midway through my stay at Jacksonville, I had learned that I would make my first carrier landings in the heart of the continent. The Navy had converted two Great Lakes side-wheeler, steam excursion vessels into aircraft carriers, by stripping their superstructure down to the main deck and fitting them out with a flight deck, arresting cables, and a tiny conning tower. The ships were named the *Sable* and the *Wolverine.* Operating out of Chicago on Lake Michigan they were safe from attack by German and Japanese submarines patrolling the seacoasts.

During flight operations, these carriers steamed up to twenty knots into the wind to produce at least twenty knots of wind over the deck. When they ran out of lake space they reversed course at top speed for an hour or two then turned into the wind again.

Sam, Vic, and I checked into NAS Glenview the same day. We got together in the BOQ and hiked down to operations to check in. Scores of aviators milled about in several large rooms, going and coming from flights or waiting to be scheduled. A PA system announced pilots' names, told them to prepare to fly and to check

The USS *Sable* on Lake Michigan was used for carrier landing qualification. Converted from a Great Lakes excursion vessel, she had side-wheel propulsion.

U.S. Naval Institute

three large schedule boards labeled Field Carrier Landings, *Sable,* and *Wolverine*. Within an hour, our names appeared on the Field Carrier Landing board. I had thought training practice was behind me, but I had to make two such practice flights at an outlying field before being scheduled to go to a ship. Sam was the first to go to a carrier. He qualified and went on leave. That night a weather front moved in and flying was canceled. Vic and I waited through the next day, watching pelting rain driven by gusty wind rake the airfield.

One day, while I waited in a group of officers for the club to open for lunch, a couple of men from my Del Monte Preflight School platoon wandered up. I greeted them and we began to exchange stories of the training program. One of them looking over my shoulder suddenly exclaimed, "For God's sake, look who's here. It's Schultz, our platoon leader at preflight!"

Schultz smiled broadly as we surrounded him, offered his hammy hand while trying to remember our names. "Hey, I remember you guys, a tough bunch to handle. Glad to see you made it. What planes are you flying?" I was pleased to see him again, a man one could admire and follow gladly.

As we chatted jovially on the sidewalk, we sensed that we were blocking other officers approaching the club. We sidled off the curb to let them pass and continued our gossiping but were abruptly silenced by a commander who had detached himself from the passing group. "Attention! Give me your names," he ordered. We reluctantly complied. "Report to the office of the commanding officer of the air station and await his return."

We saluted, "Aye, aye, sir."

I looked at Schultz, "What in hell was that all about?"

"I don't know." He shrugged.

Puzzled, we did as ordered and sat dejectedly in an office facing a desk with a nameplate that read Captain G. C. Montgomery, USN. An hour passed before a pasty-faced captain with a two-martini flush in his cheeks appeared and sat behind the desk. We jumped to attention and stood stiff as fence posts. Sweat began to trickle from my armpits and my heart thumped against my ribs. The captain looked at us as a butcher might size up slabs of beef, his hard eyes looking for the best place to start cutting. He fixed a hypnotic stare on Schultz, whom he vaguely seemed to recognize as an officer assigned to his command. "Do you officers know why you are here?"

Schultz squeaked, "No sir." And we did the same.

Getting nothing substantial from us, he growled, "What is your proper greeting when you meet a senior officer?" Ah-ha, so that was it. We hadn't come to attention and saluted him and the commander outside the club. By persistent questioning, just another way of exerting his authority, the captain squeezed a halting explanation from us in bits and pieces about our chance reunion and an apology for not acknowledging their approach. He responded, "This is a military organization, not a social club. The sooner you learn that the better." He twisted the knife, "I'll have this offense noted in your records."

By this time, I was prepared to kiss his backside if it would release us from this absurd situation. Our explanation in no way satisfied his sadistic urge to make us stand, squirm, and sweat helplessly. Finally he stopped; presumably he had some other pressing duties besides terrorizing junior officers. He sneered, looked us up and down again, and dismissed us—except Schultz. I glanced backward, furtively. Schultz still stood at attention and was gradually shrinking to the size of a regular guy.

One must suspect major character flaws in a person like Montgomery who chose to exercise his authority in such trivial and inappropriate circumstances. Screw him and screw the system that produced him. I wouldn't forget nor forgive.

Well into the second day of waiting for a change in the weather and with more of the same predicted for the following day, "Vic," I said, "let's spend tonight in the Chicago Loop. We won't be flying tomorrow anyway." He agreed and we caught a bus to the city, drank more than was wise, and went to bed late in a room in the Stevens Hotel with a view of the lake and harbor where we could see the *Sable* and the *Wolverine* moored. With the wind and rain continuing they would be there tomorrow. We were awakened the next morning by bright sunshine streaming into the room. I jumped out of bed and took a quick look at the lake. "Wake up, Vic. It's clear as a bell and the lake's choppy from a strong east wind. Damn, *Sable* and *Wolverine* are gone."

Vic groaned, "We should be in Glenview right now. Conditions are good for flight operations. The ships are probably landing planes already."

We struggled into our clothes, made it to Glenview by eleven o'clock, and rushed to the operations ready room. As we entered, our names were called on the public address system to report to the operations officer. He was in a filthy mood, "Where in hell have you two been? I've been paging you since early this morning?" Vic spoke up in his most contrite southern accent, "I hope you'll forgive us, commander; we were in Chicago all night. The weather forecast was so bad we were sure flight operations would be suspended. We were dead wrong. We're sorry. We're ready to fly."

"Sorry, hell, you were AWOL. What would happen to this operation if everyone came in late today? I'll tell you. We would miss the best flying conditions in months. I'll be submitting a report on you two to the commanding officer. While I'm preparing that, get into your planes and fly out to *Sable*."

"Aye, aye, sir." We saluted, scrambled into our flight gear, checked our plane assignments, and got into the air in record time. We were joined by a lead plane and two others and headed out over the wind-whipped lake. I could see the *Sable* wallowing east through five- to ten-foot waves, her side-wheels churning a milky, frothy wake. As we orbited her at 1,500 feet, waiting to be called down for landing, I could understand the apprehension of pilots who had landed on her. They griped that the deck was too narrow and the flight deck too short. They all found it disquieting to take off knowing that if they went into the water off the bow, those side-wheels could end their careers if not their lives. It looked a hell of a lot worse than that to me.

My radio crackled, "SBD three-zero, your flight cleared to begin landing, over."

Our leader called, "This is SBD three-zero. Roger, cleared to begin landing, out." He led the flight into the landing pattern upwind on her starboard side at 150 feet. There, I could see more clearly the height of the breaking waves, the churning side wheels, and the ominous heaving of her deck—not a pretty picture. He signaled for right echelon and we moved to his right. When due, I peeled off to the left and headed downwind. When abeam amidships, I began a left turn, losing altitude, watching the landing signal officer and trying to ignore the surging sea and heaving deck. During my approach, I received and responded to several signals from him and got a cut on my first try. I yanked back on the throttle, pulled the stick into my crotch to stall the plane. It bounced and jerked to a stop. I'll be damned! I did it!

Someone shook me. I looked up. It was a deck crewman. He pulled aside my helmet and shouted into my ear, "Are you all right?"

"Hell yes, just a little stunned by the experience."

"You're delaying operations. Release your brakes. We have to push you back to give you more space to take off." I was in favor of that.

Trying not to think about those churning side-wheels, like twin waterfalls sending a cloud of spray aft as high as the conning tower, I followed the deck officer's signals, "hold brakes," "rev-up," and "start takeoff." I released the brakes, the plane lurched forward. The end of the deck arrived long before I wanted it to, but the plane took to the air with only a minor, goosey dip toward the water. The other seven landings were easier.

My radio opened up. "Calling SBD three-zero this is *Sable*, over."

"*Sable* ,this is SBD three-zero, over," responded our leader.

"Return to air station. You are qualified." I had passed the test. Vic joined up with me and we headed for Glenview and a celebration at the club with several Seagram's Seven Crown and 7 Ups.

That flight to make eight carrier landings took less than two hours. The next morning, the operations officer announced that more landings had been made during the previous day than had ever been made in one day during the operations of the two carriers. I hoped my next assignment would be a combat squadron.

I began fifteen days of leave and set off to visit Dad in Idaho, where Mother and Rosemary waited before going on to San Francisco. As the commercial airliner droned west, I closed my eyes and relived the experience and thrill of landing on the carrier. I marveled at how the Navy had trained me to do that by hundreds of increasingly challenging steps until the final step seemed almost automatic. My thoughts drifted to what to expect between Mother and Dad after such a long separation. I guessed that it would be much as it had been for me, the little boy of the family. I would observe nothing unusual. The "adults" would have all their important interactions in private.

The flight to Idaho was a bumpy milk run. I remember only one stop, in the middle of the night. As we parked on the tarmac,

I could see the town's name painted on a hangar, Fargo, N.D., the town where I had gone through elementary school. I stared at the sign for half an hour. It had a special message for me, "Get off the airplane and look for your old friends." It would have been a crazy, disrupting thing for me to do. I stayed on the airplane and continued to the rendezvous with my splintered family.

When I walked down the ramp, I could see Dad's stocky figure waiting by the gate, dressed in comfortable outdoors clothing, his fedora squarely on his head and a cigar in his mouth. He had grayed noticeably. We exchanged our usual restrained hellos, hugs, and handshakes. That had not changed. We all have our own ways of expressing affection, and we learn to recognize and appreciate how others show theirs. He was showing his love as forcefully as he could.

I picked up my luggage and followed him to his car, a late '30s coupe, climbed in, and settled down for the drive to Wallace. "How do Mother and Rosemary like Wallace?" He grunted and puffed on his cigar, "OK, I guess, but they seem restless. It's not like San Francisco, you know. Not much to do. They don't treasure the nearness of the mountains, forests, and streams as I do. I expect they'll be leaving shortly."

"Yeah, they've been away from San Francisco for about a month, all the way to Jacksonville, then up here, and they still have a long way to get back home." I sensed "home" sounded empty to him, since he had not been home with the family for a long time. He seemed to slump a little and stared forlornly at the road for several miles. The highway curved around a mountain ridge, crossed a swiftly flowing river, and skirted a huge sparkling blue lake set between rugged forested slopes. That seemed to stir him. "Jimmy, I wish your mother liked this country the way I do."

"Yeah, me too; that's too bad. I wouldn't mind living here."

We sank into silence as the highway snaked through the mountains and into Wallace, a bleak old mining town crowded into a canyon with steep forested ridges. Dad had a small bachelor apartment, and he had rented a suite of rooms for Mother, Rosemary, and me. Mother and Rosemary had been there for a couple of days, during which they had established an amicable but restrained relationship with Dad. This détente was sustained for the several days that they stayed after I arrived. When they left, I remained with Dad for another week. It had become clear to me that Mother would never live with Dad again. I was surprised she had agreed to visit him in Idaho. She must have done it because she thought it would please Rosemary and me. It didn't. It saddened me to realize the finality of their separation. Dad was noncommittal about their relationship and never mentioned what I'm sure he knew, that their marriage had ended six years earlier.

Dad had become well established among the mining people in Wallace, Idaho, where he managed a milling operation. He was obviously proud of me, in my officer's uniform with shiny bars and wings, when he introduced me to his friends and business associates. If that gave him pleasure, the trip was well worth it. But it was not much fun. Not like being with my flying buddies. I'm certain his friends had never seen a man dressed in naval aviator's greens. They were congenial and interested in what I was doing but really understood little about how I fit into the war effort. I had no trouble answering some of their misguided questions, like "How do you like the Army?" and "Was boot camp tough?"

My old roots were dying and new ones were sinking into the future. I couldn't plan beyond joining a combat squadron and heading west to where the war was raging in the Pacific. The real action for which I had been preparing for almost two years was about to begin. I felt the need to get on with it. The uncertainty of the future charmed me and urged me forward. I left Wallace before my leave was up. Dad and I had another hug and handshake parting at the airport. I was headed for Norfolk, a reunion with Sam and Vic, and into the unknown with them.

The transient BOQ at Norfolk was crawling with officers waiting for assignments. Sam, Vic, and others from our training group from Jacksonville were there. Sam had a big surprise for us. While on leave, he had married his high school sweetheart, Bonnie Lou. We celebrated the event at the club, but it disturbed me.

I couldn't understand why he had done that. He was just twenty years old with no money or career prospects or training, except flying. For him such sensible considerations against marriage at this time must have carried no weight. Arguments in favor of it seemed to be mainly biological. The war had forced us from our homes, families, and friends and created yearnings for relationships with others to take their places.

None of us believed we would not return from the war, although we knew, of course, that pilots were killed out there. I'm sure Sam had not married because he thought he would die; more probably he had done it in a surge of romantic feeling. I wondered, had he rushed into marriage as a conscious step toward becoming an adult? I'm certain he had not thought of the sober part of marriage: responsibilities for wife and kids, bills, arguments, disappointments, and most of all, the loss of independence, all aspects that deterred me. I felt some nagging resentment toward Bonnie Lou. She had come between us, a wedge that would split him from Vic and me.

We had no duties at Norfolk except to wait until we received our assignments. That meant bull sessions in our rooms and the bar, occasional trips into town for no good reason or result, where booze cost twice as much and the locals considered naval officers migrants to be avoided. No one left the station for more than a few hours for fear orders might arrive and they would be left behind. In a few days, orders arrived. Sam, Vic, Dick, three others from our Cecil Field group, and I were ordered to NAS Wildwood, New Jersey, to join a dive-bomber squadron, VB-87.

The other three men from our group were destined never to join a combat squadron. One had failed to qualify on a carrier, one was erratic, and the other was an excellent pilot but wild. The Navy sensed they would be unsuited for carrier squadron duty. They were sent to primary and operational training stations where they would help teach others to fly. To them, it was like being sent to labor in the salt mines. The wild one couldn't resist the thrills of living close to disaster by buzzing beaches and making simulated gunnery runs on other aircraft. I liked the wild one, but I didn't understand him. I had a farewell drink with those three and tried to help them rationalize their disappointments.

Among the several means of transportation available to Wildwood, Vic and I chose to ride a passenger ship through Chesapeake Bay and up the Potomac River as far as Washington, an overnight voyage. We shared a small cabin with barely enough deck space to turn around once we dropped our luggage. It was a place for sleeping only. We roamed the decks, watched the murky water slide by, viewed the distant, low-lying, swampy shoreline until something more interesting materialized: two young, unattached women. Here was an opportunity to observe my charming and successful southern gentleman buddy operate.

He stalked them like a minister after a prosperous-looking visitor at church. He made certain they were aware of us before he uncocked his hat, straightened his necktie, assumed the attitude of a puzzled traveler uncertain of what lay ahead, and asked them a general question, "Where can we find a room in Washington? We understand it's crowded." I figured civil young women could not avoid giving some kind of an answer to a sincere-looking serviceman far from home.

"I'm sorry, we don't know Washington very well."

"We only have a day to spend in Washington. What sights should we be sure to see?" Vic asked.

They said, "The Capitol, Lincoln Memorial . . . there are tourist attractions all over the place." They began to give and take. He introduced himself and eased me into the conversation. So that was the way it was done.

We strolled around the deck with them, exchanging small talk until we "rediscovered" the bar. Vic said, "We were thinking of having a drink. Would you care to join us?" After a drink or two, we had dinner together. By this time, we had decided who would have whom. Things were going swimmingly. It was dark in the late evening when they suggested it was time to retire. They knew, of course, that we also had a cabin. The possibility of pairing-off was obvious. Vic gallantly offered to treat them to a nightcap from a bottle of Southern Comfort in our room. They demurred, but we headed them in the right direction. En route they stopped in front of their cabin, opened the door and stepped in, said, "good night," and closed and locked the door. End of lesson. We drank more Southern Comfort than was reasonable and turned in.

The next morning, we woke no wiser and less well than the night before. The ship was tied to a dock at Washington. We were the last passengers to leave the ship.

9

Joining Air Group 87

Naval Air Station, Wildwood, was just another temporary-looking facility hacked out of swampy land a few miles from the ocean. A tidal lagoon separated the air station from a sandy beach ridge on which sat the town of Wildwood-by-the-Sea. The station supported the formation and training of squadrons to fly the Navy's latest dive-bomber, the SB2C Helldiver, large, powerful-looking, and, to me, intimidating machines compared to the SBDs at Cecil Field. Vic and I found a Quonset hut with a crudely lettered sign VB87. (V—for heavier-than-air, B—for bombers). We checked in and received a cheerful welcome from Sam. "Hey, roomies, y'all look a little bushed. Was the boat ride rough?"

We moved into the same room in the BOQ with Sam and began scouting the area for entertainment. Dick bunked nearby. We four caught a bus into Wildwood, which turned out to be a favorite beach resort for vacationers from nearby cities, mainly Philadelphia. It looked promising, with the summer season just beginning. Since most young men were in the service, the vacationers were young women, frightfully outnumbering us. We couldn't fail to fall in love with a place like that. If you didn't make a connection one week, the next week brought a flood of new-comers from which to find a sweetheart for a week.

Senior officers and those with wives rented quarters off the station, as did small groups of bachelors. Those bachelors preferred the privacy and freedom to party that they couldn't have in the BOQ. We called those places Snake Ranches, suggesting wild parties involving party girls.

The commanding officer, Commander Porter W. Maxwell, USN, U.S. Naval Academy Class of 1936, was among the last officers to report. He had a reputation as a no-nonsense, stern, and aloof man. That was an understatement. He carried his slender, well-proportioned, six-foot-three-inch frame gracefully. His narrow, spare face with a full mouth, slender nose, and narrow chin made a striking impression, like the Indian warrior chiefs Sitting Bull and Crazy Horse. His eyes, large and bulging, were most impressive. When he first fixed them on me with one of his intense stares, I knew how a webbed fly must feel as the spider approaches. They were a challenge to see if you would stare back. No one did. At least I didn't. I had the feeling he made a penetrating visual evaluation and established dominance much like male dogs do when, with legs stiff, tail high, and a fixed stare, they circle a stranger. I knew I would take no liberties with him. "He's got gun-muzzle eyes and a rifle barrel up his ass," Dick said. "They're standard issue at the naval academy, you know." After a few weeks, he seemed to relax a little, but I saw no indication that he formed friendships with anyone. He suffered from the loneliness-of-the-leader syndrome.

The squadron had a different ambience than other naval units I had been in. It had a feeling of permanence that had been lacking previously; I think the presence of senior, war-experienced aviators, not as instructors but as flying mates, made the difference. These were the men with whom I would go into combat. I had been dealt cards for what could be the final time in this war, part of a hand, a low card, to be played for better or for worse. Since I would be

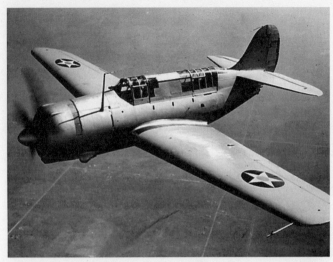

Curtis SB2C "Helldiver." The plane's electrical systems were notorious for their lack of dependability.
U.S. Naval Institute

living, playing, and flying with these men for many months, I made a special effort to fit in and maintain amicable relations with them.

We learned to know our squadron mates in the habitats of aviators: the ready room, the flight line, aloft, BOQ, the Officers' Club bar, and parties. Cliques of pilots were drawn together by flying in the same division, rooming together, having trained together elsewhere, and through similarity of rank and combat experience. None of us green ensigns became buddy-buddy with combat-seasoned senior lieutenants. There were small circles of intimate friends, like Sam, Vic, and me. On the edge of those circles were men we knew well and respected, like Dick, who had been my cadet roommate at Kingsville. Beyond that were men we had not known previously, who outranked us by too much or were not one-of-the-gang types, ones who didn't like being that kind but couldn't help it or loners who wanted it that way.

A squadron is closely analogous to a clan, the clan patriarch being the commanding officer, his elder advisers, the executive officer and senior lieutenants. Clans are held together by blood relationships and survival imperatives, a squadron by naval orders and regulations, love of aviation, patriotism, and survival. We were still individuals, who liked some squadron members more than others, but the squadron bond attached us to all men in our group and tended to shut out others.

I learned to fly the SB2C, the second plane I would fly, with only ground instructions and a cockpit checkout. This plane taxied quirkily, took off sluggishly, and landed heavily. Once in the air, it flew straight and level but seemed heavy and clumsy even when not loaded, like a boat half full of water. Adding a couple of thousand pounds of bombs in the bomb bay would certainly not make it nimble.

Most service airplanes had a hydraulic system (to actuate the flaps, wheels, propeller, and wing folding), but this plane had electrical systems notorious for their lack of dependability. They would fail altogether, or circuits would get crossed and, instead of dropping the flaps, would drop the wheels, light the bombsight, or shift the propeller to high pitch. The accumulation of reports of such malfunctions made me treat the plane with the same respect I would a snake pit.

First impressions that are negative usually moderate to acceptable with continued exposure and practice. I learned to be reasonably comfortable in the SB2C, but performed dives, takeoffs, and landings with studied caution. Some pilots outright detested the plane. We soon named it "the Beast." One detester, named Hotshot, became known for the frequency with which he would test a plane on the ground only to find some fault with it and avoid making a flight. One of his flying mates once told me that as he and Hotshot would walk toward their planes on the flight line, he could hear the wheels spinning in Hotshot's head trying to find a reason for not flying the assigned aircraft. Once in the air, Hotshot could fly all right but he commonly departed early for home for some real or imagined malfunction in the airplane.

The things we had learned to do in dive-bomber training at Jacksonville we learned again with more purpose, more attention to what would make us more effective attackers and survivors. We were assigned to a flight leader, flew on his wing, learned his idiosyncrasies, and became part of a team. Life exhausted us. Exhausted us, not from the flying but from the long hours spent in Wildwood carousing with the never-ending troops of women from beach, bar, and boardwalk (sometimes under the boardwalk, known as the "Underwood Hotel"). For couples seeking more intimate togetherness, small shingle-sided hotels flashed inviting signs Rooms, Vacancy. They didn't need to add, "no questions asked."

A favorite hangout and body shop, Lou Booth's Club, featured a stand-up comedian backed up by a black male trio who sang everything the Ink Spots ever recorded. A favorite of theirs, "I'll Be Seeing You in All the Old Familiar Places," charmed us. We hushed when they harmonized "Into Each Life Some Rain Must Fall." I'm in Wildwood again on the rare occasions when I hear it on a radio station that plays ancient music.

Such diversions kept us in Wildwood until after midnight. Reveille at 0600 and flights at 0730 were a struggle. Some of us thought breathing pure oxygen in our masks helped to push aside the cobwebs. I tried anything I thought would help. At last we were into the hard fighting for which we had been conditioned in preflight school. By midafternoon, our systems had recovered to near normal again. It only took a shower, a couple of drinks at the BOQ bar, supper, and we were on the bus for another evening in Wildwood.

This routine was more than most mortals can endure. Rick, one of our buddies from Jacksonville, continued it beyond belief. He became enamored of a singer in a nightclub who didn't finish work until 0200. He stayed in the club until then and spent an hour or two with her before returning to the air station and bed. It took a team of us to awaken what appeared to be a corpse in his bed. He eventually showed signs of life, got up zombielike, braced himself with cups of coffee and sweet rolls, sniffed oxygen for a few minutes, and seldom missed a flight. He was saved from certain physical deterioration by the move of the squadron to another air station.

At Lou Booth's Club I met Annie (or was it Helen? no matter), from an industrial town in Pennsylvania. She was vacationing with a klutzy girlfriend who owned the car they traveled in. It was clear Annie and I were meant for each other. She was petite, with smooth, dark skin and bedroom eyes. I treated her and her friend to as much beer as they wanted until, at a late hour, her friend insisted that they leave. Annie invited me to leave with them. Her friend parked on the street, said good-night, and disappeared in the direction of their hotel, leaving us in her car.

The next day I vaguely remembered Annie's name and my promise to meet her on the beach that afternoon. I found her alone looking a little pale but pleased to see me. "How do you feel?" I asked.

"OK, but my friend is mad at me."

"Oh, why's that?"

"She didn't like the white shoe polish on the ceiling above the backseat of her car."

Dick's sweetheart, Martha, chaperoned by her mother, visited him at Wildwood. I liked her and her mother, both straightforward staid midwesterners, so different from Dick's WAVE friend at Kingsville. There would be no experimenting with coital positions on that visit. I took their picture standing before a Beast, Dick's arm discreetly around her waist. I envied Dick.

Mac, a smiling fireplug of a man, with an outgoing personality and organizational ability, soon became a popular senior officer with us. He had had a tour of duty in the Pacific, flying from the old *Saratoga*, a legendary carrier to us but "Sara" to him, and had also been based in the Solomon Islands. His room in the BOQ was across the hall from ours. One evening, Sam and I met him in the hall when he was returning from a shower, a wet towel tied around his waist and his toilet kit under his arm. He smiled and said, "You guys look thirsty. Come on down to my room for a drink."

His room had two unmade beds, a dresser, and a desk cluttered with empty beer cans, glasses, magazines, and a week-old newspaper. He jerked straight the covers on one bed and said, "Have a seat. Whiskey coming right up." He tossed the towel aside, squeezed into a pair of shorts, and dug a bottle out of a dresser drawer. I noticed that nude he didn't outrank me. He gathered up three glasses, sniffed them, frowned, rinsed them in the washbasin, lined them up on the desk, and poured a couple of inches of whiskey into them. "The only mixer in this joint is water," he said. "Help yourself." We began drinking. He asked, "How do you like flying the Beast?" We both made a face for an answer. He understood and only smiled. After a couple of drinks, Sam said, "Mac, what was the scariest flight you were on in the Western Pacific?"

"Goddamn, that's easy, and it all happened because of that asshole, MacArthur," he started off. "We hated the general because as supreme commander he gave the dirtiest jobs to us, jobs the Army Air Forces were afraid to attempt, like attacking shipping in the Jap stronghold at Rabaul on the island of New Britain.

"Rabaul," Mac said, "was the most heavily defended harbor in the whole damn South Pacific. A high ridge surrounded it," he cupped his hands; "the entrance was a narrow channel," his finger tips opened a bit, "kinda looked like Diamond Head, Hawaii, but much larger and, of course, flooded. It was the main supply port for Jap forces in the Solomons and points south."

"Yeah, we know about that," Sam said, "but you were way down in the southern Solomons, how did you get way up there in an SBD?"

"It wasn't easy. The Marines and Army had captured an airstrip on Bougainville, halfway from Guadalcanal to Rabaul. We loaded our bombs and fuel at the Canal, flew up the 'slot' to Bougainville and refueled. That's where things began to heat up. The Japs had been pushed back from the field but not out of range of their artillery. They lobbed shells on us as we refueled and taxied to the end of the runway. One of our planes was hit and exploded there. The other eleven of us got off helter-skelter, like a flock of seagulls, and headed north.

"We got separated from our fighter cover, and Zeros began to attack us as we dropped through scattered clouds over Rabaul. We dove at a lousy, low angle through a hole in the clouds into fucking intense, dazzling flak from the ships and shore. I strafed a ship and skip bombed it, then hauled ass for the harbor entrance, a bottleneck, like being in a shooting gallery as one of the ducks. Only six of us got out of that hell-hole and back to Bougainville, where the Japs shelled us again as we refueled."

"Did they hit you again there?" Sam asked.

"Nah, but old Gutsy Gordon's plane died there, so only four of us straggled back to Guadalcanal. That bastard, MacArthur." I couldn't guess how I would react to a situation like that. I'd probably just follow the leader, like Mac had.

Early in our stay at Wildwood, the skipper initiated an experimental program to test the concept of skip bombing against ships. This technique was similar to skipping a pebble on the water surface, as we had as kids. It required making a shallow dive, then leveling out while skimming the water to drop a bomb that would skip once or twice before it hit the ship. Mac led one of the first practice flights in Delaware Bay with two young pilots flying on his wings. As he leveled off near the water, a wingman hit the water. The plane sank and the pilot died. The Beast had claimed a victim from our squadron. He would not be the last.

Mac felt that somehow it was his fault. It haunted him for months. Skip bombing dropped off the training schedule but the death of a squadron member lingered.

Next to flying, women were the favorite subject of conversation. Sam had a low-key way of recounting experiences with women.

"Ah had this sweet li'l ol' high school doll, Mary Belle, in Mississippi. Since there wasn't much entertainment in town we took to walkin' the fields and woods. Ah was real fond of her, and she of me, so one thing led to another. It was a whale of a lot of fun but things got outta control as we lay on the moist ground. On our walk back to town, ah could see that the back of her dress had big wet patches and so did the elbows of my shirt and the knees of my pants. When we turned down the street toward her house, we met her mother. She looked us up and down and her smile froze. She said, 'Mary Belle, come with me.' Ah've always thought, only experience coulda told her the meaning of those wet spots."

Not all squadron members shared in these bull sessions and carousing. Carl seldom mixed in. He busied himself padding his medium-size frame with rippling, bulging muscles by pumping iron and selective dieting. Alcohol he shunned. Everywhere he went in the Navy, he toted a seabag containing a hundred pounds of weight-lifting equipment. He was pleasant and friendly, but his abstinence and innocence along with his smug, indulgent smile irritated me. He had no close friends, but we tolerated his aloofness because he was one of us. To me, most men in the squadron had likable qualities, except Wayne, a large man with fat hips, a plump feminine face, and a high-pitched voice. When I shook hands with him, I instinctively wiped my hand on my shirt. He affected a pseudointellectual tone, and his attempts at joviality were off-putting and laced with bathroom humor. Still, he was one of us, so we drank with him and endured his inanities.

Seven weeks into the program at Wildwood, the Navy announced a massive reorganization of Air Group 87. The bomber and torpedo squadrons were downsized from 36 to 24 planes and the fighter squadron increased from 36 to 50 planes, the largest squadron of carrier aircraft ever organized. This change required that pilots, including me, from the bomber and torpedo squadrons be transferred to the fighter squadron stationed at NAS Atlantic City, New Jersey.

A Grumman F6F Hellcat Navy fighter.
U.S. Naval Institute

My only regret when I traded flying the Beast for the prospect of flying the Grumman F6F Hellcat, the Navy's newest carrier-based fighter, was being separated from Sam and Vic. I had preferred to fly Hellcats when given the choice, but now I had gotten into them more or less by accident.

In mid-August I packed my bags and with several other pilots rode a bus for an hour to NAS Atlantic City, where we joined our new squadron, VF87. We checked into the BOQ and the squadron. The first squadron pilot I met was Ken, my roommate at preflight school and Alturas CPT. He still had his Rolex watch and Windsor knot in his necktie. We were not happy to see each other. The next day I began flying Hellcats.

I had the usual ground briefing and cockpit checkout and was told to take a familiarization flight. I climbed into the cockpit for the first time in my flight gear, ready to take her up for a spin around the area. An enlisted plane captain stood by ready to load a starting charge, which resembled a shotgun shell, into a hinged breech below the engine. I signaled him to load it. When he stood clear, I pumped the priming pump a couple of times, set the propeller in low pitch, moved the throttle to a start position, glanced up to be sure the man had stood clear, and engaged the starter. The propeller revolved and stopped. The man ducked under the engine and shoved another starting charge into the breech. He stood clear and made a pumping action with his hand. I hit the priming pump a couple of times and engaged the starter again. The propeller swung around a couple of times and stopped. The plane captain stood staring at me with his hands on his hips and disgust on his face. He ducked under the engine again, loaded the breech for the third time, and then scrambled onto the wing and glanced into the cockpit. He took a deep breath, reached in, turned on the ignition switch, and without a word dropped off the wing and signaled me to start. The engine roared into operation.

Now that the tough part of operating the Hellcat was behind me, I taxied out and took off. I felt at home in the Hellcat on the first flight, nothing quirky about it. It did what I wanted it to do and promptly; there was nothing sluggish about this cat. I was relieved not to be responsible for a crewman riding in the backseat as in the SBD and SB2C. Alone and in control, much as I had been since my family had broken up, was the way I wanted it. Flying a fighter aircraft in a combat squadron suited my nature. I had developed a loner's attitude toward my personal destiny, but enjoyed my friends and did my share to advance the interests of the group.

It took a while to discover who was commanding this outfit. There was a gaggle of senior lieutenants but none above that rank that I could recognize in their unirank flight gear. If the bomber squadron had a full commander, surely there must be an officer of similar rank in this enormous squadron. Not until we had a squadron meeting did a tough-looking lieutenant emerge from the crowd and begin directing affairs. He maintained a wholesome give-and-take attitude with other squadron members, an improvement over the autocratic leadership in the bomber squadron.

The squadrons of Air Group 87 neared the end of their formative stage at separate air stations. The other recently transferred pilots and I were trying to catch up with the rest of the fighter squadron by becoming familiar with the Hellcat on frequent formation flights, both day and night, and intensive field carrier landing practice. It was a hectic time, combined with drinking and hustling women in clubs along the boardwalk in Atlantic City.

In mid-September, like migrating birds, all squadrons left their nesting sites and headed south for the winter. We fledglings followed our elders, in their late '20s and early '30s, to NAS Oceana, Virginia, near Norfolk, where the three squadrons would begin to function as a unit and I would join up again with Sam and Vic.

In late August 1944 the Allied armies had broken out of the Normandy beachhead and were approaching the Seine and Paris. In the Pacific, the New Guinea and Solomon Islands campaigns were completed, and key islands in the Marshall, Gilbert, and Marianas Islands had been captured. Allied invasions of the Philippines were in the offing.

Wildwood and Atlantic City had been my first extended experience with wild dissipation. Near its end, I felt a nagging dissatisfaction with myself, remembering the phony exhilaration of booze, smoke-filled clubs, inane talk, sloppy dancing, clumsy caressing, tacky hotel rooms, empty late-night streets, roaring hangovers, and worries about VD. I wasn't very good at it, and on balance it had been not much fun, not nearly as stimulating and fun as flying. Occasionally, in sober moments, I wondered why I kept it up. It must have had something to do with hormones and peer group approval that made us squirm so pathetically in the sweaty grip of war.

10

Routine Training Flights

The air station at Oceana, like many others sited in the southern piney woods, had expanses of asphalt, look-alike buildings, rows of airplanes, a traffic control tower, all surrounded by a high wire fence. In nearby Virginia Beach, a popular summer resort, the crowds were gone and beach businesses boarded up. Norfolk, although close by, was still a rotten liberty town, crawling with men in uniform. There would be no rollicking Wildwood or Atlantic City experiences here.

For me, there were some bright spots. Sam, Vic, and I checked into the same room in the BOQ and picked up our friendship where we had left off when I had been sent to the fighter squadron. I discovered that Joey, a schoolmate from Montana, also a naval aviator, was stationed nearby. We had played together on football and basketball teams. He and his wife, whom I also knew well, were living in an apartment in Virginia Beach. I would see them often.

The squadron ready room was a Quonset hut. That's where we hung out when not flying. Its battered tables and desks, tacky overstuffed sofas, folding chairs, schedule board, lockers for flight gear, and a wood-burning stove showed the wear and tear of many squadrons and the hundreds of aviators who had come this way. Ragged copies of naval safety publications were scattered about, and official notices were tacked to the walls not occupied by lockers. Acey-deucey, a backgammon-like game, the traditional naval aviator ready room board game, was in progress much of the time. I could never get interested in it.

The skipper and the administrative officer each had a cubicle in a corner, which they called offices. Standing-room-only squadron meetings were held there. During cold weather, with windows and doors shut, the woodstove fired, and with most of the seventy-five pilots smoking, it became a suffocating cave. The bar in the Officers' Club was where most serious decisions were made and unofficial business transacted. It has been claimed, face-tiously, that air stations everywhere were constructed around a desirable spot for the Officers' Club.

Here I learned about an organization I had previously been unaware of: commander, Air Group 87, and his staff. The commander coordinated the operations of the three squadrons and linked to higher command. Part of our flying time was devoted to simulated attacks coordinated by the air group commander. But the bulk of our time, still, was preparing for carrier qualification in the Hellcat and practicing bombing, strafing, and rocket attacks.

In early October, we learned that the air group would embark eventually in the USS *Randolph,* CV 15, a large *Essex*-class carrier being fitted out nearby. The commissioning of the *Randolph* on October 9, 1944, at the Norfolk Navy Yard had all hands present, including Air Group 87. She was an awesome war machine. The ceremony of commissioning on the flight deck, replete with speeches by high-ranking officers, martial music, fluttering flags, and row on row of officers and men, was appropriate to the occasion. She would carry us, and our planes and ordnance, to within range of the enemy and launch us. We would be the tip of the spear. It began to sink into my consciousness that I was in a responsible and personally dangerous position. I had volunteered for this; I had learned too late the military dictum, "never volunteer for anything." But none of us then would have given up our place in this venture.

The crash of a dive-bombing Hellcat near Manteo, North Carolina, that killed a squadron pilot was the beginning of a series of disheartening and sobering tragedies while at Oceana. Late one afternoon Vic came into our room and asked, "Have you heard about your friend Leon?" I had a sinking sensation. Leon was an ensign who had become a good friend, a slender, sensitive man, the type that seemed to belong in school bands, English clubs, and honor societies, not in a fighter squadron.

"He crashed on an attempt to land on *Charger.*"

"Oh, too bad! Too bad! How did it happen?"

"He made a low approach and the landing signal officer gave him a wave-off. Leon applied power but couldn't clear the stern of the ship, slammed into the transom, slid, and cartwheeled across

The USS *Charger* (CVE-30) jeep carrier was used to qualify pilots on Chesapeake Bay.
U.S. Naval Institute

the corner of the deck and into the water, almost took the signal officer with him."

The squadron sent out several planes to search the crash area, a futile but necessary gesture to show we cared and that we could count on the squadron to do the same if we went into the water. It had a bonding effect on us.

A few days later, a dive-bomber pilot I always thought of as a "wild one," frustrated at not being a fighter pilot, made a simulated gunnery run on an Army Air Forces twin-engine bomber, not noticing that the bomber had a target sleeve on a steel cable in tow. He hit the cable, fatally injuring himself. My friend Dick had the sad duty of accompanying his sealed casket to his next of kin.

As if that were not enough, my Montana friend's wife called and tearfully reported that Joey had crashed while practicing field carrier landings at night. His plane hit the ground in swampy woods and burned. The difficult terrain delayed rescue efforts. He was still alive when they rushed him to the Norfolk naval hospital in critical condition from broken bones, internal injuries, and burns. I visited him in the hospital several times. He was bandaged like a mummy and could barely speak, a mumbling wreck of what had once been a vibrant man. He would remain in the hospital for months and eventually be discharged, severely disabled, from the Navy.

Before Oceana, death had been an abstraction, a condition distant and not related to me. I had been aware of pilots who had been killed but none had been more than a name, except Paul. Now, squadron men, friends, suddenly had disappeared, their belongings gone and their names removed from our rosters, as movies that had ended their runs, their reels packed off into the unknown, to be replaced by others with different names.

My feeling of invulnerability eroded. What had been a lark took on a palpable sense of lurking hazard. The realization that most accidents were caused by pilot error focused my thoughts on anticipating threatening situations and thinking through actions I would take to counter the most obvious hazards, like engine and structural failure. In most cases, it would be a decision of whether to stay in the plane or bail out, and whether there was time to communicate. I began reading with more care Navy publications that described accidents, trying to gain safety for myself from the misfortunes of others. Still, I tried not to dwell on things negative, knowing they distracted my mind from the demands of flying.

Early in World War II the expression "routine training flight" began being used in military aviation press releases to describe the circumstances under which an aviator was killed. The repeated use of that expression inadvertently indicated the hazardous nature of flying for the military. If so many fliers were killed on "routine" flights, what must be the rate of loss on "nonroutine" flights?

We had many of both kinds of flights in Hellcats out of Oceana. A routine type was to fly to a bombing range near the beach at Manteo. There you could test your bombing proficiency by dropping miniature bombs on a bull's-eye while ground observers recorded where the bombs hit. Each flier received a numerical score for a series of drops. This exercise brought out the competitive instincts in even the most jaded flier. One of those routine-training-flight releases to the media described how our promising young aviator had died at Manteo. He didn't recover from a dive and hit the ground near the bull's-eye. He and his flying mates had made trivial wagers on the bombing scores that would result from the flight. Some suggested that these wagers encouraged unwarranted risk-taking and were a factor in the accident. Such bets were thereafter forbidden. Perhaps other factors were more important.

A few days after that tragic accident, my four-plane division took off in the early morning for that same target at Manteo. The air was cloudless and calm. As we joined up and gained altitude over Currituck Sound, we roused clouds of migratory waterfowl that swirled in the sunrise against a backdrop of the distant ocean. Details of the marsh vegetation on the broad, swampy coast faded to gray green smudges on a mirror of calm water as we climbed and droned uneventfully south. I was contented, happy even, lulled by the serenity of nature's display. Too soon, we were in the landing traffic pattern at Manteo. Our stop there to load miniature bombs was routine. We took off, climbed, and began bombing. While pulling out of several dives, I scanned the ground looking for some sign of where my squadron mate had crashed. I saw none.

We completed the bomb drops, joined into formation, and climbed to 15,000 feet for the return flight to Oceana over the broad, shallow Albemarle Sound. I relaxed, held my position in loose formation, and enjoyed the view. Our leader's voice came on the radio, "We'll make a practice dive on Target Charlie; it's the white pylon at the edge of the water." We all gave him a thumbs-up. He signaled for an echelon-right formation. We began our high-speed run-in, accelerating to 275 knots and peeled off at 12,000 feet in another routine training dive. As the last plane, I had to make a hard roll to the left until I was inverted, hanging on my safety belt, my head tilted far back to see the target. I reduced engine power, pulled the nose down into a steep dive, and maneuvered my bombsight onto the target.

The target rapidly filled the sight. At 4,000 feet and air speed above 350 knots, I pressed the bomb release to simulate a bomb drop and eased back on the stick to terminate the dive. The centrifugal force suddenly increased, driving me into the seat with unusual force. Color faded, my view narrowed, and everything became gray, like twilight on an overcast sea. Suddenly it was black. I was diving down a dark shaft.

I didn't worry; this had happened several times during other maneuvers. Lacking sight, messages from my other senses became accentuated. The vibration of the Hellcat became more violent and its frequency increased; the engine became surprisingly loud; the pitch of the whistling slipstream increased alarmingly. My heart began pounding. Still no need to worry; sight would return soon, as it had before. Darkness continued; I increased backpressure on the stick, still with no sign of light. Fear stabbed me in the belly when suddenly my mind imagined the ground coming up to meet me. I must do something different, but I had only one option. I relaxed the backpressure on the stick and pushed it forward. That steepened the dive and was completely alien to my flying instincts. Within seconds, light flooded in from the end of the shaft. My reflex-driven arm leveled the wings, canted 30 degrees to starboard, and continued the dive recovery. Twiggy branches and leaves of marsh vegetation flicked by in sharp relief. I was out of the dive and climbing slowly, dazed. I shuddered and felt weak and empty when I realized how near the ground I had to have been to see details of the vegetation. My flight leader's voice in my earphones calmly said, "Join up, join up. Let's go home."

That focused my thoughts. My eyes darted to the instruments. I needed more power and altitude. The g meter showed I had pulled out at eight times the force of gravity. I scanned the sky and saw the other planes far away, north of me and higher. I longed for the slim comfort and security of being with them and in a few minutes powered my way into formation. Had anyone noticed my errant dive? Would the flight leader chide me for my tardy join-up? Such thoughts temporarily pushed those other frightening what-if thoughts to the back of my mind.

The postflight exchanges among the pilots in the ready room resulted in no embarrassing criticisms of my flying. No one seemed to have noticed my "deep dive" or late join-up. To them, it was just another routine training flight. I lacked interest in my bombing scores, and their talk about lunch made me queasy. What I wanted was a martini.

Should I volunteer information about what I had experienced? Should I open the door to unwanted discussions that might suggest deficient airmanship? I remained silent for the time being. That day I made a vow to myself that I would never black out again, a promise that I kept.

No doubt I was in a turn when I began that pullout, and back pressure on the stick did not pull me out but kept me in a tightening spiral. The expression "graveyard spiral," which I had heard described in bull sessions, fit what had happened to me, except for the "graveyard." I believe my squadron mate, who crashed at Manteo, had an experience like mine. I can visualize him pulling back on the stick in blind desperation, as I had, until he hit the ground. Another few milliseconds, and I would have been the subject of a press release about a routine-training-flight fatality.

Now that the danger of blacking out was forever chiseled in my mind, how could I prevent it? Blacking out is known to result when centrifugal force, which develops while recovering from a dive or in a tight turn, drains blood from the head. The solution to this problem was, of course, to prevent the loss of blood to the head. I had heard the problem discussed by others and remembered that one recommended action was to tighten your abdominal muscles, thus restricting the movement of blood out of the upper part of the body. In addition to using this technique, I began to bend as far forward as possible during a pullout. That, I reasoned, would tend to move the blood from the back of my body to the front, instead of from the top down, and thus prevent, to some extent, loss of blood from my head. The issuance of antiblackout suits shortly thereafter helped me to keep my no-blackout vow.

Antiblackout suits were snugly fit, of lightweight fabric, with embedded inflatable bladders. The bladders were located on the abdomen, thighs, and calves. A hose connected them to a source of compressed air that was automatically introduced when a certain amount of centrifugal force was sensed. The inflated bladders pressed firmly against the lower body, trapping the blood in the upper body and head, thus inhibiting downward drainage of blood. Antiblackout suits must have saved dozens, perhaps even hundreds, of lives.

Oceana was not all gloom and terror for Vic. His hometown sweetheart came to visit him for a few days starting in midweek, accompanied by her mother, of course. It was a sedate, homey visit, with hand-holding strolls along the beach and boardwalk, visits to the air station, dinners at a nice restaurant, topped off by a good-night kiss before he boarded the bus to return to the air station. That was until Friday afternoon when Sam received a phone call at the BOQ from his and Vic's Tennessee girlfriends. They were in a hotel in Virginia Beach, panting for a weekend of partying.

The situation looked manageable until it was discovered that the two girls were in the same hotel and a few doors down from Vic's sweetheart and her mother. Sam dashed into town to find Vic and warn him of this awkward situation before the two parties accidentally met. He took Vic aside to try to resolve the situation without hurting anyone's feelings. Their solution was to call me and invite me to take Vic's place for the weekend. I declined the kind offer out of fear of being inadequate to the situation.

They had to tough it out for the weekend. The strain was mainly on Vic. Sam kept the girls occupied during the early evening until Vic could discreetly part from his sweetheart and rendezvous with Sam and the girls back in the hotel. These furtive comings and goings were nerve-wracking for Vic but highly amusing to Sam and me. When it was all over, Vic was drained and fidgety after what he said was the most stressful weekend he had ever spent. He was ready to go to sea for the calming effects it can sometimes bring.

By November the air group and the *Randolph* were ready to begin working together. The *Randolph* had been shaken down sufficiently in coastal waters to start landing and launching aircraft. On the day we were scheduled to join the *Randolph*, clouds hung low and wind raked the field as the air group's planes took off to rendezvous with the ship thirty miles offshore. At the *Randolph*'s location, a gale blew. The low-hanging clouds and sea were lead gray except for whitecaps streaming like manes of stampeding stallions on fifteen-foot waves. The seas moving in different directions produced an ugly, confused surface.

The ship rolled and pitched ominously, unable to steam a steady course upwind. Landing operations would probably be messy. I would have voted in favor of calling off the affair, but no one asked my opinion. The ship's captain and the air group commander would make that decision. Meanwhile, we continued to circle and circle and circle, a hundred planes at one thousand feet, between the opaque overcast and the churning sea. After the decision had gestated for an hour, it was finally born. "Aircraft return to the air station and try again tomorrow." No flier raised an objection.

Under more favorable sea conditions, I made several landings on the *Randolph,* and eventually most of our aircraft landed on her and she came to port. The other planes were loaded by crane at dockside. The air group moved aboard and made ready to start a lengthy shakedown cruise at an undisclosed location.

II

Shakedown Cruise
aboard the USS *Randolph*

Close-up at dockside the *Randolph* looked like a gray wall standing in murky harbor water. That she displaced 33,000 tons meant nothing to us. The dimensions that interested us were her flight deck length, nearly 900 feet, and its width, 100 feet; these were near the upper limits for vessels transiting the Panama Canal. She had a crew of 2,400 or more, plus the air group.

I lugged my baggage up the gangway to the hangar deck. It looked like a hangar, with Hellcats, torpedo-bombers, and dive-bombers crowded together. The bulkheads and overhead were patterned with pipes, wires, and beams. Sailors in dungarees hurried about, and mechanics worked on the airplanes. Through huge open doors in her sides I could see daylight. A PA system clicked on, and a bos'n's whistle echoed through the ship, followed by, "Now hear this! Now hear this! Sweepers, man your brooms, clean sweep-down fore and aft. Sweepers, man your brooms, clean sweep-down fore and aft." No one seemed to respond but I assumed sweepers and brooms were swinging into action somewhere.

I dropped my bags at the desk of the officer of the deck, a lieutenant wearing an armband with OOD printed on it. I saluted him and said, "Ensign Vernon, reporting aboard with Fighter Squadron 87."

He returned the salute, "Welcome aboard. Stack your bags out of the way and go to the fighter squadron ready room for instructions." He spoke an incomprehensible seaman's jargon that included topside, oh-two deck, ladder, aft, athwart ship, starboard, port, amidships, and scuttlebutt. "You can't miss it," he ended. I think he was showing off, not really being helpful but trying to confuse me. He succeeded. It made me think of my first day at college or an unfamiliar metropolitan railroad station.

I tried following his smart-ass cryptic directions with no luck. Asking directions from a couple of officers, I finally found the ready room and checked in with the squadron officer of the day. He had a list of room assignments. I retrieved my baggage from the hangar

The USS *Randolph* (CV-15). Her flight deck length, nearly 900 feet, and width, 100 feet, were near the upper limits for vessels transiting the Panama Canal. She had a crew of 2,400 or more, plus the air group. *U.S. Naval Institute*

deck and hiked forward to "officer country," a maze of twisting passageways and dead ends in the fo'c'sle, known to a landlubber like me as the "forecastle." Vic, Sam, Dick, and two other junior officers from the air group were already there. Double bunks, a table, lockers, a desk, and several chairs comprised the furnishings. The rooms had curtains, not doors. Showers and heads (toilets) were nearby, down a passageway. It seemed reasonably comfortable.

Forward of our room, watertight doors opened onto a deck, open all around the bow but with the flight deck above, like a covered patio. It looked out on a crowded harbor where great gray ships rested at docks, cranes were silhouetted against the sky, and small craft crisscrossed the open water. The *Randolph* lay motionless as a rock. I checked out the wardroom; it contained long linen-covered tables and a small lounge area. Some tables had discreet signs reading Senior Officers. The mess stewards were black.

The following day, in a flurry of last-minute loading, the *Randolph* prepared to depart for her shakedown cruise. On the dock, sailors gave good-bye hugs and kisses to wives and girlfriends and waited in lines at telephones to make calls home. I mailed short letters to Mother in San Francisco and Dad in Idaho. I could tell them little beyond that we were going to sea, I would be out of touch for a while, and I loved them. We didn't know where we were going but were scheduled to return to Norfolk. Moistened by drizzle, on November 22, the *Randolph* slipped her ties to land and, nudged by tugs, eased into Hampton Roads behind two destroyers, her antisubmarine escort. Together, we steamed out of Chesapeake Bay past Cape Henry and shaped a southeasterly course to take us into the Gulf Stream and east of the Bahamas. The destroyers cruised a mile ahead, straddling our track, coursing hounds sniffing for submarines.

I gazed aft over the gloomy restless sea, watching the land fade, a sight that raised vague fears and solemn reflections. I had entered a new phase of life. Far from land, the captain announced that we were bound for Trinidad and that flight operations would begin the next day.

Within hours, we entered the Gulf Stream. No change could have been more welcome to lift my spirits after days of cold, somber weather in Norfolk and the drama of watching my country fade into the mist. Clear blue water glinted cheerfully in the gentle sun; balmy air brushed my hair as I followed the flights of flying fish that took to the air as we glided toward them. Around us, the serene, timeless sea spread unbroken in all directions, cutting us off from cares of the land and focusing our attention on cares of the sea, a vast blank slate on which to scribble our perishable prologue. The ocean lifted the stresses built up during the hectic days before the ship sailed and enhanced my awareness of the uncertainties and adventure that lay ahead. We flashed more smiles and stepped more lightly as we harmonized with the ship-navy of decks, bulkheads, overheads, ladders, and hatches, no longer land bound in dreary look-alike air stations.

Before flight operations began, the ship's plane-handling officers briefed us on flight-deck procedures. We would taxi, take off, and land in confined spaces, often perilously near the deck's edge and other airplanes. A wrong move could result in injuries to deck men, the plane, and the ship, and be potentially fatal to us. The procedure for a catapult launch was the most unfamiliar and complex. The powering mechanisms for the catapults, one on each side of the forward flight deck, were below slots in the deck. A bridle was fitted to hooks that projected a few inches above the deck. Following hand signals from a deck crewman, we taxied to the position where the bridle was attached to hooks under the wings.

Then the catapult officer gave the "rev-up" signal, circling his hand above his head with the index finger pointed up. You advanced the throttle to maximum engine power and checked the magnetos. If they checked out OK, you nodded, locked your throttle hand and the elbow of your stick arm to avoid jerking the throttle and stick back, pressed your head against the headrest,

A Hellcat Navy fighter plane ready for catapult launch.
U.S. Naval Institute

and prayed. It had to be a short prayer because moving your head back said "I'm ready."

The catapult officer threw his arm and body forward and down, like a pitcher throwing a fastball, to signal the triggerman to catapult the plane. The plane, a pebble in a slingshot, snapped in three seconds to seventy knots before you began to fly the plane.

The second day of operations, dive-bombers took off for the first time. In the ready room, I heard the Klaxon sound, announcing trouble: a plane in the water. I scrambled to the flight deck. "What happened?" I asked a somber officer staring toward the bow.

"A dive-bomber took off, climbed straight ahead to about 800 feet. Suddenly, its left wing went down and it dived into the water, the damnedest thing I ever saw."

The ship slowed and passed the wreckage, a stone's throw to port, where I could look down at it. I could see only one wing and the tail. The pilot and aircrewman were below the surface. The wreck drifted astern, where a plane-guard destroyer drew alongside. Within minutes, the plane slid beneath the choppy sea, a winged coffin gliding two brave young men into a vast, timeless tomb countless fathoms deep.

Within a few minutes, I learned that the pilot had been my buddy Dick. The shock brought tears and sorrow. His first and last flight from the *Randolph* ended in death. Disbelief stunned me; how could an intelligent, methodical, strong, and smoothly coordinated man like Dick be the victim of that bizarre crash? If any of these qualities of his could have prevented the crash, he would have used them with skill as great as anyone's. He and his crewman must have been victims of a catastrophic mechanical failure that Dick realized too late for them to bail out. The Beast had killed them. From then on, the thought haunted me: what chance do we of lesser skills have to survive this war?

I stood there on the flight deck in the warm tropical sun, thinking of the families of Dick and his aircrewman. They would receive telegrams beginning, "We regret to inform you that your son . . ." and be cast into mourning, the object of their twenty years of loving and nurturing obliterated in an instant. They would never fully recover. I remembered well his fiancée, Martha, at Wildwood, a fresh, bright, sincere, and strong young woman. She still had a life ahead of her, but it wouldn't be with Dick. The best of us needed good luck to survive. The inept, wild, careless, or unlucky flier was marked for extinction. Dick had been an unlucky one.

The PA system clicked on, a bos'n's whistle shrilled through the ship, "Now hear this! Now hear this! The smoking lamp is out on the main deck level and above while refueling aircraft. The smoking lamp is out on the main deck level and above while refueling aircraft." The ship picked up speed and continued on course.

I helped gather and pack Dick's gear for shipment to his family. His empty bunk remained a silent but eloquent reminder of the dark side of flying and war.

We continued south, beguiled by the tropical climate, the sun high, hot, and dazzling, the air soft and humid, but the slumbering sea reminded us of its domination by effortlessly rolling our huge ship. We were a mere mite on the heaving breast of a great, implacable, eternal creature. It had taken two of our finest as its own. I feared they would not be the last, for death has a thousand doors but none so wide as the sea.

We had suffered casualties, but the effort had to continue. After a discreet pause to permit the shock of the crash to subside, flight operations continued. They did so without serious incident as we skirted the Bahamas, transited the Mona Passage between Puerto Rico and Hispaniola, and crossed the Caribbean Sea to Trinidad. Between Trinidad and the Paria peninsula of Venezuela are the Dragons' Mouths, narrow entrances into the Gulf of Paria, where we would shake down. These entrances were tightly guarded to ensure that no German submarines could enter. The Gulf is eighty miles long and thirty miles wide. The weather was muggy and sunny, and the sea oily calm. Here, the ship and aircraft began to function like a well-drilled team.

Perhaps the most important activity, and the most difficult, was to reduce the time between landing aircraft. By now, we had made enough landings to be comfortable and confident, so we could begin stressing the timing of landings. One key to such timing was the interval at which the planes broke out of formation to be properly spaced. When planes entered the landing pattern heading upwind, they formed a four-plane echelon right with wheels down. If there was a plane ahead of the division, the leader had to peel off to fall behind it with the correct spacing. The other planes peeled off at about six-second intervals. On the downwind leg, you had to go over the checkoff list to prepare for landing, flying slowly, at an altitude of about one hundred feet. The altimeter was useless, so you flew at the height where the horizon intersected the ship's superstructure, about fifty feet above the flight deck. The point where you began a 180-degree turning approach to the deck was a matter of judgment, taking into consideration the speed of the ship, wind speed, and the distance from the ship. Here seat-of-the-pants flying took over.

We soon learned that "sucking flat in the groove," that is, ending our turn far aft of the ship, raised the danger to everyone involved, because the bulbous nose of the Hellcat blocked your view of the landing signal officer and the deck, a sure way to get a wave-off and an ass chewing. You had to be in a turn throughout the approach to see the signal officer. Ideally, the plane should be about twenty feet above the deck and come out of its turn with level wings almost at the stern. When a "cut" was signaled, the pilot jerked the throttle all the way back, and stalled the plane with the stick in his crotch. After the "cut," the plane was out of control until the tailhook caught an arresting wire and jerked it to a stop. The deck crew ran to the tailhook and disengaged it from the wire. A plane handler signaled to roll smartly forward of the barriers that had been lowered. The barriers consisted of cables stretched across the deck to prevent an out-of-control plane from careening into other planes. The pilot stopped the plane, and a crew folded the wings and directed the plane to a parking spot or an elevator that lowered it to the hangar deck.

The times between landing were all recorded. Those who habitually had long intervals or received wave-offs were admonished and given tips on how to improve. Ship's personnel recorded and reported the average landing interval to the squadron commanders. As time passed, the intervals became shorter and the wave-offs less frequent.

The *Randolph* steamed into the roadstead off Port of Spain, the capital of Trinidad. The PA system clicked on: "Now here this! Now hear this! The anchoring detail lay forward to anchor. The anchoring detail lay forward to anchor." The ship stopped dead in the water, the anchor chain thundered out of the hawse pipe, and the anchor dove in like a sounding whale. All hands were scheduled for liberty. That meant drinking in the Navy club or higher-class joints that featured calypso music in the city. Street vendors hawking worthless trinkets constantly harassed us. Rum, the drink of the island, had been immortalized by the Andrews Sisters' rendition of a song of that era, first played in the rum mills of Port of Spain, "Drinking Rum and Coca-Cola." One line said something about the mothers and daughters working for the Yankee dollar. They didn't earn dollars from anyone I knew, though a "change of luck" would have been welcomed by some of us.

After we had been in Trinidad a few days, a rumor seeped down that a fourth squadron of flying Hellcats would be formed in the air group. This would be the second such change. The first had sent me and others to the fighter squadron. This rumor gained substance when pilots from the bomber and torpedo squadrons were sent to Waller Field on Trinidad for a checkout in the Hellcat.

When our shakedown cruise ended, we had another liberty in Port of Spain. Sam, Vic, and I spent a day there drinking and dinging around. In the early evening, we wandered down to the boat dock. A boat waited there, but they were not offering rides to anyone in our group. In a few minutes, Felix Baker, captain of the *Randolph,* arrived and boarded it, the captain's gig. He waved the group of us to come aboard. Vic, with inhibitions erased by island rum, shouldered through the crowd close to the captain and asked in a loud voice, "Hey, Felix, where are we going when we leave here?" the question foremost on everyone's mind. Felix took the question with good grace and said, "I know but I can't tell you now." Such informal address and such an audacious question could be cause for discipline, but Captain Baker just laughed it off.

Early the next morning, the bos'n's whistle sounded. "Now hear this! Now hear this! The anchor detail lay forward to weigh anchor. The anchor detail lay forward to weigh anchor." We sailed from Port of Spain, transited the Dragons' Mouths, picked up our destroyer escorts, and headed north toward Norfolk. When Trinidad had sunk into the sea, the captain came on the PA system with a little speech. "Last night a young officer asked me where we were going when we left Trinidad. I couldn't tell him then but I can tell you all now. We are headed for Panama."

And so we knew. The ship changed course to port and headed west, where the flat sea met the dome of the sky along an ever-retreating line. This change of plan stirred consternation in the ranks, for now wives were stranded in Norfolk, expecting their husbands to return, and girlfriends were deserted forever by their suitors. One or more automobiles that probably would never be recovered had been left parked at the air station. The Navy seemed indifferent to these inconveniences. We stayed the course. The problems on land must somehow resolve themselves.

The ship had to pass a final test. The engines had run for more than thirty days and were "broken in." The time had come to see how they responded to high power demands and what speed the ship could make. While the engines' rpms gradually increased, vibration increased, the wake boiled, and loose objects rattled. At maximum power, she shook alarmingly. The engines continued at maximum power for half an hour; the top speed attained was thirty-two knots, close to forty miles per hour.

We had begun a series of voyages west through the infinite sea toward the war zone half a world away, more than twelve thousand miles. We had adapted to shipboard life and slipped comfortably into the ship's transiting routine: reveille at 0600, breakfast at 0630, muster in the ready room at 0700, the first flight off at 0800. When not on the schedule, we had few obligations and were challenged to fill the hours with other than sack time. The best time filler turned out to be bridge. Among the squadron's junior officers, I alone knew how to play the game. Before long, I had taught its rudiments to half a dozen of my buddies. Vic quickly demonstrated his aptitude for the game, and we became regular partners for the duration of the war.

The ship maintained combat air patrols (CAP), fighters stationed above the ship, as she would in the war zone. Although the threat from enemy aircraft was zero, the pilots and air controllers got good practice. We also made simulated attack approaches on points of land and against the air defenses at the Panama Canal Zone. I thought of it as a pleasure cruise without women, but with the excitement of flying.

Liberty in Panama differed little from Trinidad, mainly booze, broads, and street vendors. The passage through the canal entertained me far more than liberty. The *Randolph* slipped through the locks with only ten feet to spare.

We departed Panama on the twenty-third of December and shaped a course for San Francisco, eight days and nearly four thousand miles away. En route, training flights again "attacked" simulated targets along the coast. I flew on one such flight that targeted Cabo San Lucas, the southern tip of Baja California. On that cloudless day with visibility unlimited, the *Randolph* with her two escorting destroyers transited one hundred miles off the coast through a slick, dead-calm sea. For several miles, we could see our ships clearly, but as the distance widened only the wake remained visible. At fifteen thousand feet over Cabo San Lucas, I could still see the wake, at least one hundred nautical miles away, a V pointing north, a useful bit of information to tuck away, a phenomenon unknown to me until then.

Off southern California, our aircraft were launched for the last time. Their destination: NAS Alameda, on the east shore of San Francisco bay. Pilots who were not flying ashore, like me, rode the ship through choppy gray water with green mountains to starboard, like stage scenery, into San Francisco Bay. I was coming home. I drank in the sight of a hundred familiar landmarks as we steamed through the bay: the bridges, Alcatraz and the other islands, the city's hilly skyline, the Ferry Building where I had entered the Navy, the East Bay cities, Berkeley and the university with its campanile, and the many piers, like fingers jutting into the bay. We docked in the Hunters Point Naval Shipyard, the place I had worked as an engineering assistant before I went on active duty. On the way to a Navy bus stop, I took a leisurely stroll about the yard. The changes since I had left made it difficult to recognize the structures I had worked on. It was now almost completely operational, crowded with ships, sailors, and civilians. I noticed an engineer sighting through an instrument. As I moved closer, a wave of pleasure washed over me. I recognized my old boss, the one who had hired me off a crew of gandy dancers more than two years earlier. I tapped him on the shoulder. His head snapped up with a grunt of irritation. I said, "Hi, Hal, its good to see you again." It took him a few moments to recognize me as his former rodman. His frown magically spread into a broad smile as he shook my hand.

"For God's sake, is it you, Jim? Where in hell did you drop from?"

"Just in from Panama and points east on the *Randolph* now at that dock over there that you and I laid out a couple of years ago."

"I'll be damned, and the Navy turned you into an officer." He smiled slyly, "Do I have to salute you?"

"No, at ease, Hal. I'll overlook that formality as long as you address me as 'sir.' " We had slipped into the lighthearted banter we had used during the months I worked for him. It gave me a warm feeling that the smile never left his face.

"Where are you headed?" he asked.

"West. Haven't you heard there's a war going on out there?"

"You don't say. Is that why there are so many sailors and ships around here?"

"That's the reason. Sure enough."

We exchanged news about our families and other workers I had known there. When we began to run out of things to talk about I said, "Well, Hal, I have to catch a bus into the city. It's great seeing you again, and thanks for all the things you taught me while I worked for you. I'll see you after the war."

He became serious, "Thanks, Jim, look me up after the war. I'll find a job for you so we can work together again." He shook my hand, patted my shoulder, looked me in the eye, and murmured, "Take care of yourself." I turned away and headed for the bus stop thinking that I could use more friends like that.

The rumor of the creation of a fourth squadron, Bombing-Fighting 87, in the air group became a reality. Its formation required the transfer of pilots from the other squadrons and from a replacement squadron. This realignment of Air Group 87 and others that would follow us into combat was in response to changes in the tactical situation in the western Pacific. Allied forces were closing in on the Japanese home islands. An invasion could not be far off. The main factors causing these changes were

1. Reduction of the Japanese navy and merchant marine to impotence (decreasing the demand for specialized aircraft capable of delivering bombs and torpedoes)
2. The rise of attacks on our fleet by suicidal, piloted aircraft (kamikazes) (increasing the need for more fighter aircraft)
3. Recognition of the fact that fighter aircraft could perform the dual role of dive-bomber and fighter
4. The planned invasion of Japan (massive numbers of ships of all kinds would require greatly increased numbers of fighters to stop the kamikazes)

As a result of these developments, Air Group 87 disembarked the *Randolph* and another fully trained air group went aboard. Our newly formed bomber-fighter squadron could not have operated with the rest of the air group, and the ship, without substantial training. The new squadron would fly Hellcats, and Vic and I transferred into it. Sam remained in the bomber squadron.

We hung in limbo, knowing that a crucial and perhaps the most dangerous part of the war awaited us off Japan.

12

Voyage to Hawaii

With regret, I said good-bye to the *Randolph,* a congenial home. She wouldn't take me into combat after all. Everyone in the air group had leave over New Year. Men scrambled to find transportation for visits home and to communicate with their wives and families. Those who remained in the Bay Area took rooms in the BOQ at NAS Alameda. I called my family in San Francisco and they took me home, three rented apartments near Golden Gate Park.

Sam and Vic had met Mother and Rosemary at Jacksonville and they joined us for family partying. Sam's newly acquired wife, Bonnie Lou, arrived within a few days. Our family shifted about and freed an apartment for their second honeymoon. When Bonnie Lou left, Vic and I occupied the apartment. By then, Mother had been attending San Francisco State College for more than a semester. She gave me a copy of her class schedule so Vic and I could visit her on campus. When we arrived, she sat in an English class. We cautiously entered the room and took seats in the back row, not unnoticed by the class of young women. Mother was old enough to be the mother of even the professor. We were an unfamiliar species to them. Naval aviators didn't frequent that habitat. Most were down on Powell Street boozing in the Yankee Doodle Bar or at the Top of the Mark.

When the class ended, the young women drifted out slowly; a couple hung around apparently wanting to be introduced to us. But Mother was anxious for us to meet her professor. The professor brushed the chalk dust from her hands and smiled graciously as Mother, beaming with pleasure, introduced us. I put on a mock-serious face and asked, "Does Mother do her homework on time, and do you ever have to send her to the dean's office for disciplining?" She laughed, put her hand on my mother's shoulder, and assured me, "Your mother is one of my best behaved and most scholarly students." Mother bore this in blushing good spirits, no doubt recognizing my spoofing was to remind her of the many times she had had stormy sessions with school principals because of some misbehavior or scholastic deficiency on my part. Plainly, she loved the life of a student; my financial support had made her happy with so little effort.

Shortly after I arrived in San Francisco, I called Dad. He dropped activities at his home in Idaho and caught a train for San Francisco. He found his three daughters congenial but Mother polite and formal. In her new independence as a student realizing the dream of her life, she refused to be deterred from becoming a teacher. Dad stayed only a few days. I wouldn't see him again or experience his awkward expressions of affection until the war ended. I felt intensely sorry for him.

One evening, I left the Yankee Doodle bar and wandered down Powell Street toward Union Square. As I waited for a cable car to clang clang clang past, I felt a tap on my shoulder and heard a familiar voice say, "Hi, you old pud. Thought you'd have puddin' killed yourself by now." Only his uniform had changed, to bell-bottoms and a squashed white hat. I shook his hand and impulsively hugged his shoulders. "It's great to see you, you cynical old fart. Come on into Lefty O'Doul's. I'll buy you a beer."

"I usually draw the line at drinkin' with puddin' officers, but I'll make an exception for an old friend."

We took stools at the bar, ordered beer, and griped and laughed about preflight and flying at Livermore. He didn't want to talk about his life as an enlisted man and showed no interest in where I'd been or my present status. My uniform told him all he wanted to know. That left little more to say. We seemed to have ended up in different worlds, separated by an invisible wall. He began to pensively scrape the ashes from his cigarette on an ashtray and stare into the mirror behind the bar. I idly slid my beer back and forth in a puddle on the bar, unable to find anything to say. We couldn't recapture the rapport we had felt only a year earlier. "I've got to get back to the base," he mumbled; "got the pudding duty." I paid for the beer and we sidled outside, stood on the corner looking blankly at each other, then in opposite directions. He tentatively shook my offered hand. "Stay out of the pudding drink."

"I'll try. Take care of yourself." He turned his back and drifted slowly toward Market Street.

My leave orders had me report to Alameda for further instructions. After I checked in, a yeoman told me I must go to NAS Vernalis, where the squadron had been commissioned. That meant checking out of the station I had just checked into and riding a Navy bus sixty miles to the east. That sounds simple, but the procedure required at least ten stops where information had to be provided and signatures obtained. Near the end of the day I arrived at Vernalis, only to learn that the squadron had been transferred to NAS Watsonville, another sixty miles away. Because it was late, I slept in the BOQ. The next afternoon, I finally caught up with the elusive squadron. Lieutenant Commander Haas, a transferee from a replacement squadron, directed the commissioning and training activities until Commander "Muzzle-Eyes" Maxwell, as Dick had called him, from the bomber squadron returned from leave to take command.

Things were chaotic in the ready room, where new men from a replacement squadron and old faces from the bomber and torpedo squadrons were busy getting acquainted with the Hellcat. We were scheduled to move to Alameda in a few days; from there we would fly to San Diego. After I had hung around the ready room for an hour, the exec told me to go back to Alameda since I was already experienced flying the Hellcat. That meant busing to Alameda again. I must have set some kind of record for checking in and out of air stations, four in three days.

We stayed only briefly in Alameda. While a large group of us waited on the tarmac for an airplane to San Diego, a clutch of enlisted men a short distance away also waited to go somewhere. One of them broke from the group, walked toward us, and singled me out. "Hi, Jim, I haven't seen you since high school in Helena. I'm Russell Cross." I had played basketball with Russell on the B-team in 1938, coached by Hank Secrest.

"Hey, Russ. Good to see you. I saw old Hank Secrest at preflight school about a year ago. He was then a full lieutenant. It was a great treat to see him. Do you remember his reading you the riot act because he caught you smoking?"

"Hell, yes. My ass still burns when I think about it." He laughed.

"How do you like the Navy, Russ?"

"I like it a lot because we're always packing our seabags and going somewhere." That attitude seemed to be natural for him. He had been restless and out of touch with school. In a few minutes, his group began marching away. We hastily shook hands. He looked me in the eye and said, "Take care, Jim. I'll see you back in Helena." He picked up his seabag and ran to catch up, then turned and waved. I waved back, wondering if I would ever see him again.

We flew to North Island Naval Air Station, San Diego, where we and the fighter squadron would board a jeep carrier (a small freighter converted to a carrier) the USS *Copahee,* also known as a "Kaiser Coffin," to sail to Hawaii. I had flown aboard jeep carriers, but she looked shockingly small compared to the *Randolph*. Hellcats for delivery to Hawaii packed her flight and hangar decks. "She looks top-heavy and slow," Vic said, "like the buses in Panama with passengers clinging to the roof." All junior officers from both squadrons, some sixty of us, were sardined in a large forward compartment below the water line. That place looked like what it had been, a cargo hold. Bunks stacked three and four high made me think of a mausoleum. Every time I turned over in my bunk, I invariably bumped the body above. The larger men had to slide out of the bunk to turn over. I liked being small.

The *Copahee* shoved off from San Diego on January 21, 1945, and shaped a course for Hawaii. A bold northwest oceanic swell, born of storms in the far North Pacific, lifted, rolled, and plunged her in a staggering cadence as she plowed patiently through them, a fragile clot of determination. She steamed unescorted at twelve knots, actually a thousand zigzagging courses designed to confuse the aim of enemy submariners wanting to torpedo us. We would be confined in her for eight days. Two days out of port, we caught the northeast trade wind on our stern.

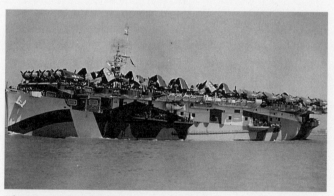

The USS *Copahee* (CVE-12), a jeep carrier known as a "Kaiser Coffin," was used to transport carrier aircraft in the Pacific.
U.S. Naval Institute

To prevent our demise from boredom, we were assigned to assist the ship's crew on the deck and bridge. The airplanes on the deck had to be guarded at night to prevent theft of the valuable instruments in the cockpits, mainly the clocks, by the crew. Members of the ship's crew and enlisted men from the squadrons guarded the planes. It was like letting the fox guard the hen house. We were assigned four-hour watches to check on the enlisted men, not easy since we sailed blacked out. The enlisted men might be anywhere among the black planes with folded wings. Tie-down lines made footing treacherous, and propeller blades made heads vulnerable, hard-hat country for sure.

After spending much time searching for one enlisted "guard," I heard snoring from an enclosed area of the catwalk, a walkway along and below the edge of the flight deck. I turned on a small flashlight to find a man sleeping like a babe. I nudged him hard with my toe and his eyes opened. "Are you Jones?" I asked. He slouched to his feet, "Uh huh."

I remembered the part of "Rocks and Shoals" I had learned in preflight school about the penalty for sleeping on watch. I growled, "You were sleeping on watch. You know the penalty for that is death, don't you?" He straightened up a bit and said, "I warn't sleepin', just checkin' my eyelids for leaks."

I thought that an imaginative defense, worthy of recognition, so I asked, "Did you find any leaks?"

"Nah, black as the inside of a billy goat."

"OK, up on the deck and do your duty." He stumbled off and I never saw him again.

Watches on the bridge required only that we stay awake and scan the sea for anything unusual. Faint red lights illuminated the instruments. I had entered a hallowed site. Ghostly watch-standers resembling priests and acolytes studying and revising sacred scriptures moved silently, their cigarettes aglow, whispering, checking the instruments, changing headings, and writing in the log.

We steamed hour after hour "down hill" in the six- to ten-foot following seas of the trade winds. Every few minutes the ship changed course 15 to 30 degrees, and after a few zigzags she would be back on course to Hawaii. On some headings, the *Copahee* only pitched, but on most she tossed in a lusty roll. My sea legs were not found wanting.

The moon rose on our stern, shining alternately dimly then brightly on the rounded, ceaseless waves, all else black save light from the distant stars. The ship slogged on relentlessly while I swayed in Whitman's cradle endlessly rocking on a voyage from hypnotic to torporous. Meanwhile, the ship steamed on her voyage to Hawaii, rocking and rolling until the islands rose from the sea, none too soon to suit a hundred aviators. We rounded Diamond Head, where, like wary watchdogs, small harbor security craft sniffed us from stem to stern, then as antisubmarine nets were opened we slipped into Pearl Harbor and docked at Ford Island.

Our combat veterans had funneled through there, going to or coming from the Pacific theater. But to the rest of us, Hawaii still evoked images of hula dancers, palm trees, Dorothy Lamour, and Pearl Harbor, once the blunted leading edge but now the trailing edge of a war gone west. Sunken ships there scarred the body and pride of our nation. I thought of the hundreds of men trapped in those hulls. What had been their final thoughts? We were on our way to repay the insult manifold, but nothing could bring them back.

We had scarcely adjusted to steady footing on Ford Island when Vic and I climbed aboard an aircraft going to NAS Kahului on Maui. Among the passengers were two Navy nurses with whom Vic was quick to get acquainted. Surprisingly, I got along quite well with the less attractive of the two. Prospects for some feminine company on Maui looked good until we stood up to disembark. She towered over me, well over six feet tall. She gave me a small amount of encouragement, but she was too much woman for my callow tastes. Vic, a low-key sexual conquistador, had found a steady lady friend for the duration of our stay on Maui. Some guys have it and some don't.

13

Night Field Carrier
Landing Practice

I had arrived in paradise for the second time; the first had been Santa Cruz, California, when I was in junior high school. These places had three things dear to me: the ocean, palm trees, and sunshine. In this paradise, we transferees from the fighter squadron would suffer another long, largely repetitious training syllabus aimed mainly at pilots who had not previously flown the Hellcat. Together, Maxwell, the skipper, and Haas, the executive officer, had the needed experience to train this new type of squadron. Maxwell had combat experience in the Solomon Islands flying dive-bombers and had headed a dive-bomber training program in Florida before he had become commanding officer of VB-87 at Wildwood. Although I didn't know it at the time, as a fighter pilot early in the war, Haas had fought at Coral Sea and Midway where, flying F4Fs, he had shot down six enemy aircraft, earning two Navy crosses. He had survived several water landings in disabled planes. We were lucky he flew on our side.

VBF-87 was among the first bombing-fighting squadrons in the Navy. With that distinction came the problem of determining to what extent the Hellcat fighter could play the role of dive-bomber. We were, reluctantly, in the forefront of aircraft tactics. The Hellcat developed excessive speed in a steep dive, great for shaking a Zero off your tail, but that diminished bombing accuracy and required a bomb release at a higher altitude to permit recovery at a reasonably safe height. To slow the Hellcat we practiced diving with landing gear in a trail position, with flaps down. This worked mechanically, but introduced some quirky and scary flight characteristics that met with pilot resistance. We also feared that damage to the hydraulic system might force us to fly home with wheels and flaps down. We tacitly agreed that in combat we would dive the Hellcat clean and fast and get the hell out of gun range.

Learning to dive-bomb the Hellcat cost us the life of Art Koontz, a highly respected pilot. A flying observer, Sid, witnessed the accident. He saw Art's plane begin its dive at a noticeably steeper angle than usual. It picked up speed rapidly. Art apparently recognized this unusual situation and began pulling out. Vapor trails poured off his wingtips and tail surfaces as he hauled back on the stick. A piece of the left wingtip ripped off with a folding-over motion and hit part of the plane's tail assembly as it flashed past. The plane snapped into a violent spin, continuing its steep dive. It left fluttering behind what looked like large pieces of metal "confetti" drifting toward the water. Bailing out was Art's only hope. He didn't make it. The plane spun into the sea.

Sid was required to tell and retell his story to the skipper and a representative of Grumman, the builder of the plane. They doubted Sid's account that the wingtip had torn off, a serious matter for Grumman and us. Grumman declared that it had never happened to a Hellcat, and Sid said he had seen it happen, a classic Mexican standoff until searchers at the crash site found the wingtip in a location that proved that it had detached before the plane hit the sea. That put Grumman on the defensive. The facts came out, based on research of the plane's service history. The failed wing had experienced damage previously and had been repaired by the Navy. Grumman could still claim no Hellcat wing failures on any factory-produced wings. Despite these findings, enthusiasm for dive-bombing the Hellcat diminished.

A few days later, the squadron gathered in the station chapel to honor Art's memory, dead from a mechanical failure. It could have happened to any of us. No tears were shed. The outside world saw only sad faces and restrained actions that covered our grief and anger. The chaplain made appropriate remarks about heroism, the afterlife, and rededicating ourselves to the just crusade in which Art had fallen. A bugler sounded taps. With taps echoing in our heads, we wandered out of the chapel and back to our quarters, broke out a bottle of wine, and drank a silent toast to Art. Flight operations began on schedule the next day. Within a week, a replacement pilot arrived. The Navy had done its best to make us whole again.

Air group doctrine required that pilots be qualified to land on a carrier at night. This became a high priority in the new squadron, since many had not done this, and I was one of them. Special training called "night field carrier landing practice" was required. The hazards of landing on an aircraft carrier during daylight had satisfied my appetite for living dangerously. The prospect of landing at night contained no element of aviation romance. As romance faded, mystery took its place.

Training for night landings at sea began with practice landings on the airfield, where small lights outlined the shape of the carrier's deck. Lt. Donald Elder, our landing signal officer in charge of training, briefed us on the flight routine and the safety measures he would have in place. He also needlessly reminded us of the hazards of flying low and slow at night. With illuminated wands, he would stand on the corner of the lighted outline and wave signals as we approached. He ended the briefing with, "If there are no questions, I'll see you out on the field shortly. Good luck." I hoped it took more than luck.

As a key safety measure, he stationed a crew under the flight path at the final turn before landing. This crew, using a powerful searchlight, illuminated the bottom of each aircraft as it approached the landing area to determine whether the wheels were down and if the flaps were in position to land. If they were not, they fired a Very pistol, which cast up a brilliant red flare telling the pilot to abort the approach, and they warned Lieutenant Elder to signal that plane not to land. That system of safety checks was foolproof, but not ensign-proof. I flew in a group of six Hellcat fighters to make a series of touch-and-go, field carrier landings during that moonless night. We spaced ourselves in a racetrack flight pattern less than three hundred feet above the ground and began making landings. I made three satisfactory approaches and landings, and began to gain a feeling of confidence.

My next approach, also satisfactory, earned me a brisk "cut" from Lieutenant Elder, a mandatory signal to land. I obediently intended to cut the power, but some mysterious force caused my hand to apply full power and I began to climb. I was shocked; why the hell did my hand do that? The lieutenant would certainly fire some verbal flak at me for such flagrant disobedience. This discomfiting thought was pushed to the back of my mind by the need to fly the aircraft. I groped for the wheel control lever, found it, and applied pressure upward to retract the wheels. It refused to budge. I jerked it, still no movement. No wonder, the wheels position indicator showed that the wheels were retracted! It suddenly came to me: I had not lowered my wheels and had refused to make a wheels-up landing that would have badly damaged the Hellcat and possibly injured or even killed me.

I had, without knowing why, refused to execute Lieutenant Elder's order to land. His safeguards to protect the pilot and plane had failed. Why had he and his crew not seen that my wheels were retracted? Why had I, not knowing my wheels were retracted, refused his order to land? Their "human error" is, perhaps, easier to understand than the mystery of why, without conscious reason, I disobeyed his signal, thus avoiding a dangerous crash for me and saving him personal and professional anguish.

When I had completed the final practice landings, I had time to think of input to any discussion of the incident. I taxied and parked the Hellcat on the dark tarmac, walked to the ready room, took off my flight gear, and waited warily to see what developed. In a few minutes, the door opened and Lieutenant Elder came in. He paused, blinking while his eyes adjusted to the light, then glanced searchingly about the room. When he saw me, he stopped searching and came directly to me with a questioning expression on his face.

He began tentatively, "Jim, were you flying Hellcat number 63?"

"Yes."

"On one approach I gave you a cut but you didn't land. Right?"

"Yes"

"After I gave you that cut I saw that your wheels were not down. What was going on?"

Trying to keep a straight face I said, "I was just running a check on the effectiveness of your safety procedures."

His face and eyes registered disbelief. I knew he would reject the idea that an ensign would dare run such a check. My expression slowly changed to something I hoped showed apprehensive amusement and said, "Don, I'm just needling you. But why didn't you and your crew see my wheels weren't down?" I could see that he was struggling with his emotions. He was grateful that I had averted a potentially tragic accident and appalled that he and his crew had failed in their responsibilities. My seeming casualness bewildered him. I sensed that he would be grateful if we kept this incident to ourselves.

He said, "Jim, I don't know why our standard safety procedures failed. I'm sorry."

"Don, I didn't know my wheels were up and I don't know why I failed to comply with your order to land."

Startled by these revelations, disbelief again showed on his face. He exclaimed, "Surely you must be kidding!"

"No, I've never been more serious in my life."

His expression changed from disbelief to confusion. He shrugged and walked away, shaking his head, as mystified as I. We never mentioned the incident again.

Once a pilot had survived night field carrier landing practice, a test at sea soon followed. A jeep carrier, the *Shipley Bay*, steamed from Pearl Harbor to the sea north of Maui where pilots of Air Group 87 would demonstrate their recently acquired competence in night landings. North of Maui is the windward side of the island where the northeast trades blow continuously, most of the year at fifteen to twenty knots, generating a white-capped sea with waves averaging six to ten feet. The logistics of the situation dictated that six or so Hellcats were flown to the *Shipley Bay* for use by a relay of pilots who would fly the same aircraft after each group had made their qualifying landings. The other pilots needed to be flown to the ship and the qualified pilots back to Maui. VT 87's torpedo bombers provided this shuttle service.

Al Cassidy, my section leader, and another pilot and I were assigned to ride to the *Shipley Bay* in the rear compartment of a torpedo bomber. Not bad duty. This would be the first time I had ridden as passenger in a carrier aircraft. I grumbled, "What, no stewardess service?"

"Nah," Al answered. "This is a fly-by-night airline."

We could see nothing but black outside until the pilot made some power and altitude adjustments. We hunched down to look out through a small window. "I see the *Shipley Bay*," Al said. "She looks like a pig romping in a mud wallow."

I recognized the preparations for landing, hydraulic squeaks as flaps lowered and wheels thunked down and left turns in the carrier's landing pattern. We were near wave tops on an approach, our running lights reflected on the waves. So far so good. At the expected time of the "cut," the pilot applied full power, a wave-off. Oh well, it can happen to the best of pilots. We got a close-up glimpse of the ship as it passed below us. Again I heard the convolutions of power changes and hydraulic sounds required to make another approach. From our poor vantage point, the approach felt OK, but the landing signal officer thought otherwise and he signaled another wave-off. As the carrier passed beneath us, Al said, "We were too high." Approach number three seemed like the previous ones and also resulted in a wave-off. Al rolled his eyes, "This guy is goosey." Approach number four produced yet another wave-off, ditto numbers five and six. Al groaned, "Hang on, they're going to have to shoot us down." I had seen enough of this machine. Let me out.

Approach seven didn't seem any different from the others, but we received a "cut," landed, and jerked to a stop. In unseemly haste, we jumped from the plane and, without looking back, ran across the pitching deck to the safety of the conning tower. The landings in Hellcats we had yet to make turned out to be anticlimaxes.

Although we flew six or seven days a week, recreational activities of aviators continued as always, drinking and partying at the Officers' Club, in the BOQ, and at bars in the nearby town of Wailuku. Men, from the Navy and the Fourth Marine Division in a camp a few miles away in the foothills of Mount Haleakala, greatly outnumbered the available women. Realistically, they were not a factor for most of us. We seemed to have an insatiable need—pathetic, some would say—to cram in a maximum of those recreational activities in anticipation of a long period of isolation aboard a ship.

One evening, I received notice from the station gate that a friend waited there to visit me. I walked to the gate to find Moe, a high school friend from Helena, Montana, then an enlisted Marine from the Fourth Marine Division. He had two buddies with him. I took them to the BOQ, gave them a couple of drinks, and talked about school days and their experiences in the service. It became a little strained, since we had lost contact for several years and had little in common except high school acquaintances. His buddies enjoyed the booze but squirmed at being entertained in officer country. They stayed only an hour or two. Knowing that good booze was difficult to find and expensive, I gave them a fifth of whiskey before they left. Moe returned a couple of times, motivated, in part, I think, by the whiskey I could provide at low cost. We left shortly thereafter and I never saw him again.

While I was on Maui, my brother-in-law Bob, Rosemary's husband, now a Navy chief petty officer, was transferred to Kaneohe Naval Air Station on Oahu. On my day off, I would fly a squadron airplane to Kaneohe to visit and to bring him a bottle of whiskey. Those flights took me along the north coast of Molokai, where from a sheer cliff more than two thousand feet high several waterfalls tumble into the ocean, but only after a rain. At other times, the falling columns of water break into a misty cloud that wafts away before reaching the ocean. One of the sublime sights in nature.

On one visit, Bob told me his unit would move to an island in the western Pacific. He didn't know to which island, but he had a list of about ten that were probable destinations. We thought it might be possible to get together out there. We compiled a list of the islands, giving each a code name, the name of a large American city. When he knew his island destination, he would write to me using the assigned code name in a context that I would recognize as unusual. I could then refer to my list to determine the name of the island. I put the list in my wallet with only a faint hope that I would ever use it.

We would not get away from Maui without another fatal crash, the result of a midair collision when the propeller of one of our planes struck and disabled another plane. The plane tumbled into the ocean ten miles offshore. Joe O'Connell, the pilot, didn't bail out. He had no chance to survive that crash. He sank in deep water with his plane. The other pilot landed safely but was shortly transferred out of the squadron. We were called together for another memorial service that twinned the one we had held for Art. Two more replacement pilots joined the squadron. I wondered if I could ever adjust to those sudden changes of old familiar faces for fresh eager ones.

Al crashed in frightening circumstances while making a night landing at a field on Molokai. He mistook two rows of lights for the runway and landed on soft ground between the runway and the taxi strip. His wheels sank in, causing the plane to nose over on its back. Al, trapped in the cockpit, hung upside down while emergency crews rushed to help him. The most frightening aspect of the situation was that the plane's gasoline tanks ruptured and high-octane aviation fuel flooded over him. One spark would have made a torch of him, the airplane, and the rescue party. He endured this for an hour before being rescued, suffering only scratches, but the gasoline caused his scalp to peel as if he had a super case of dandruff.

In early May 1945 the squadron received the orders we'd been waiting for: board the USS *Ticonderoga* in Pearl Harbor, an *Essex*-class carrier identical to the *Randolph*. Before we left Kahului, Air Group 94 arrived to take our place. After several drinks at the club, we all converged in the mess hall in two lines. Our line began drunkenly chanting, "You can have it, ninety-four, we don't want it anymore." They responded, "We will take it, eighty-seven, this to us is seventh heaven." We left the next day and boarded the *Ticonderoga*. She would take us to war far to the west, where I would experience the ultimate trial, combat.

14

Into Combat aboard
the USS *Ticonderoga*

The *Ticonderoga* lay at dockside, Ford Island, in Pearl Harbor when we flew in from Maui. Here, at last, the ship that would carry us into combat, a thing of grace, utility, power, and anticipated adventure. She had arrived from Bremerton Naval Shipyard on Puget Sound only days before, where she had had damage repaired from two kamikaze attacks off Formosa: a battle-tested ship and crew. Large ships like the *Ticonderoga* have often been described as floating cities, but they differ from cities in many ways, the most obvious being the all-male adult residents. The *Ticonderoga* made me think of anthills, termite mounds, and gopher villages. Like them, most of the life was "underground."

We moved aboard. Sam, Vic, and I shared a three-man room, an improvement from the *Randolph* that reflected our small amount of seniority over the new pilots who had joined the squadron in California and Maui. They occupied what became known as Boys' Town, a large compartment sleeping a gaggle of junior officers. Our compartment was spare but adequate. Besides the three bunks and chairs, it contained a built-in desk with a safe.

In the safe, we stashed the only valuables we had brought aboard, a case of 100-proof whiskey. Alcohol, of course, was prohibited, but the squadron administrative officer took booze orders from anyone who wanted it brought aboard as "squadron gear."

Once we settled into our room, we were irresistibly drawn to the flight deck where we would perform our most stressful activities. There, a small group of us stood admiring the view and the deck conditions. The ships and aircraft destroyed by the previous air group were recorded on the superstructure as rows of silhouettes of ships and Japanese flags for airplanes. A hard act to follow. What it didn't show were the aviators who didn't return, lost to the enemy and the sea, and the 175 ship's crew members killed by the kamikaze attacks.

Nearby, a cluster of deck crewmen looked us over. A tall, spectacled sailor detached himself from the group and came toward us. There was something in his build, walk, and posture that looked familiar. We parted to let him pass, but he stopped in front of me and said, "Hi, Jim, remember me? I'm Malcolm Streeter from Helena." I certainly did remember him; he played center on our high school basketball team. I had not seen him for five years. Except for the Navy dungarees he had not changed much. We spoke of our former schoolmates whose locations he knew. He brought me up-to-date on news of Helena and continued to feed me news of the town while I was on the ship. When the kamikazes had crashed on the ship, many of his deck crew buddies had died. He had been eating lunch belowdecks.

I had again been touched by the goodwill and warm feelings that old friends and acquaintances like Malcolm projected when I met them in unusual situations after long separations. I guess we all feel better and more secure with familiar faces and places, and tend to remember the positive and forget the negative. This chance encounter illustrated again how sharing the same hazardous situation or facing a great adventure binds people together.

On May 7, 1945, without fanfare or weeping, the *Ticonderoga* shoved off from Ford Island, slid down the channel through the antisubmarine nets and into the offing, where a two-destroyer escort waited. We were bound for Ulithi in the western Caroline Islands, three hundred miles south of Guam, to join a task force. We steered southwesterly toward the Marshall Islands, with the destroyers off the bow, the trade winds astern, the sun high to port, and confidence in our crew. We were catching up with the war at twenty knots. Flight operations began the next day. For us, it meant combat air patrols where no enemy planes had flown for more than two years. We were headed for a warm-up attack at Maloelap Atoll where, on Taroa Island, Japanese were still holed up in a bypassed airfield that, in aerial photographs, looked like the cratered face of the moon. They still had ammunition for their antiaircraft batteries and much practice shooting at airplanes like ours, flying from carriers headed west. We would not be the last.

The Japanese probably won that engagement. No discernable damage was done by us. We just added craters upon craters. The

The USS *Ticonderoga* (CV-14) was an *Essex*-class aircraft carrier. She shoved off from Ford Island on May 7, 1945, bound for Ulithi and Okinawa. *U.S. Naval Institute*

Japanese scored a few hits on our aircraft, only one serious. Bateman's craft staggered back aboard covered with oil. His plane lost power; he thought he'd have to make a water landing, but the engine, for no apparent reason, regained power and brought him back. The experience stimulated those who hit the island. They returned flushed and talkative from the excitement. For me, it had been a dull combat air patrol. With all planes back aboard, the *Ticonderoga* steered again for Ulithi through the eternal sea.

During daylight, we flew continuous eight-plane CAPs over the *Ticonderoga* and her two destroyers. One afternoon, I flew the eighth plane in the last flight of the day. After four hours of grinding in circles on station at ten thousand feet, with the sun half below the horizon, we were ordered to land. The ships prepared for our landing by turning into the wind, headed away from Ulithi. We knew this course should be held for the shortest possible time. We dropped down in a high-speed spiral, broke formation, and formed the landing pattern. The flight leader's job was to time his landing at the instant the ship completed its turn into the wind, a difficult maneuver that required experienced judgment of time, speed, space, and relative motions of the ship and plane.

The sun, meanwhile, had passed vertically through the horizon, as it does in low latitudes, making twilight almost nonexistent and night nearby. As the last plane in the flight, I knew that any delays could mean I would land in the dark. This unattractive prospect and the decreased light had already raised my tension level. Still, there appeared to be nothing but routine landings by the other planes. Six planes were aboard and the seventh in the final approach. I prepared to land: wheels and flaps down, tail hook extended, engine controls checked, canopy locked back, and shoulder straps locked. My air speed and altitude were in the right range, and my spacing behind number seven adequate. He got a "cut," landed, and arrested. I continued my approach with him still in the arresting wires. I thought, "Get your ass out of the way." He didn't move. The landing signal officer waved me off.

I added power low over the ship and gained altitude. I glimpsed the deck crew scurrying about the stalled plane. I groped my way into the landing pattern for another approach. Again I went through my checkoff list and tried to size up the situation on the deck. In the failing light, I couldn't see the deck clearly. I could only make another approach and hope for the best. As I closed on the ship, I saw the plane moving. But could I land? No! I got another wave-off.

As I repeated the maneuvers to prepare for yet another approach, feelings of loneliness and discomfort set in. Three ships with three thousand men aboard were steaming in the wrong direction waiting for me to come to roost. Dark crowded in. These feelings intensified when my radio spit out "THIS IS THE AIR OFFICER. EXPEDITE LANDING!" I had never received a more superfluous command. Anger welled up. What an insensitive bastard. Did he think I liked being up here alone in the dark, tired, with a sore bottom from four hours of flying in formation? I mentally gave him the finger. It didn't put me in a relaxed attitude for another approach, only upped my stress level. I thought of my junior high school coach who told me as I went to bat that he would kick me off the team if I didn't get a hit. I didn't strike out this time: the deck cleared, I got a "cut," thumped to the deck, caught a wire, and jerked to a stop.

It had been a stressful incident only for me and a slight inconvenience for a few men involved in deck operations. The rest of the ship's crew was locked in a daily routine orchestrated by a few top officers and executed through a chain of command down to the lowest ranking deck-swabber. One could appreciate the truth of the cynical evaluation of an unnamed sage who described the Navy as "a system created by geniuses to be operated by morons."

The system worked. Those of us on the receiving end of the ship's services had meals and rest on schedule, information on demand, completely equipped airplanes on schedule, and any physical need satisfied on request. We had not the vaguest idea of how any of this was done. We were like passengers, but passengers that provided the reason-for-being of the great ship. Without us, the ship was impotent. Without the ship, we were impotent.

As we neared Ulithi, I saw an immense cluster of ships apparently anchored in mid-ocean. Not until we were hard upon them did I see white surf on the reef of Ulithi atoll and its tiny low-lying islands. The *Ticonderoga* slowed, slid past antisubmarine nets and patrol craft through a narrow channel, and anchored among the largest fleet of fighting ships I had ever seen. We had arrived at the fringe of war, some eleven thousand miles from the beginning of our westward journey, our shakedown cruise at Trinidad, but with still more than a thousand miles to go to the present hot spot, Okinawa.

Ulithi was no south sea island Eden, just a calm, protected harbor large enough to moor a thousand ships. A mile or two from us, I could see an island with a tiny patch of palm trees. I understood there were other islands out of sight, one called Mogmog, well known to those who had been there before. It supported a large boozing site. We would not have the opportunity to visit Mogmog because the *Ticonderoga* departed after two days, with many of the other ships, to form Task Group 38.4 under Rear Admiral Radford, part of the Third Fleet, with Admiral Halsey commanding.

On May 24, in single file, the stately fighting ships steamed slowly through the gap in the reef. One by one, they broke into the open sea, their natural habitat. Destroyers and light cruisers led the way, forming an antisubmarine screen, followed by the battleships *Wisconsin* and *Missouri* and the battle cruisers *Guam* and *Alaska*. The core of the striking force, the *Essex*-class carriers *Shangri-La, Yorktown,* and our *Ticonderoga,* and the light carrier *Independence,* steamed into the center of the task group, surrounded and protected by the two score and more ships stationed as much as three miles from the center. It was a stunning display of highly organized, purposeful power at the end of our nation's reach. Aviators would provide the punch that could project that power over the horizon, hundreds of miles beyond those fingertips. The heaving of our huge ship on the ocean's breast reminded me that the eternal sea's power, now slumbering, could at any moment rouse and nullify our proud efforts.

The thought of the spirit and mighty organization of the nation that had produced these weapons, trained these men, and coordinated their movements awed me. The task group moved with the deadly purpose and grace of a predator stalking distant prey, now Okinawa. Ulithi disappeared astern; it would soon be a backwater of a war that had moved northwest. We would not see it again.

We had learned to operate with one carrier and two destroyers; now we had to work with three other carriers and a fleet of ships. The task group steered a northerly course and cuffed Guam with a simulated attack while our Hellcat fighters maintained continuous defensive combat air patrols at several altitudes. The task group then headed northwest toward Okinawa and the real war. We were ready.

The battle for Okinawa had been in progress for some time. Okinawa is a long, narrow island, with a slender waist midway along its length. Our amphibious force had landed there. The Japanese army had retreated toward the south, where they were putting up stiff resistance. The Marines had captured an airfield at Yontan, in the narrow part of the island, and were conducting air operations coordinated with those of the Navy. Hundreds of American ships hung on anchors inshore west of Okinawa. That was the tactical situation on the ground in late May 1945 when our task group arrived. The task group stood off one hundred miles east of the island and began air operations. VBF-87 and VF-87 Hellcats began flying combat air patrols over the task group and barrier patrols along the Nansei Shoto (Ryukyu Islands), a chain between Okinawa and Kyūshū.

At this stage of the war, the Japanese were launching kamikaze attacks by aircraft against our ships off Okinawa. Since the pilots had received minimal training in navigation or anything else, they took off from airfields in southern Kyūshū and most flew southerly along the Nansei Shoto, navigating visually from island to island until they sighted the American ships off Okinawa. Then they dived to their deaths. Hellcats on barrier patrols were stationed at several altitudes thirty to fifty miles north of Okinawa along the island chain and elsewhere around the island, where they could intercept and shoot down the kamikaze aircraft before they sighted our ships. Stationed in the same areas were squadrons of three or four "picket" destroyers whose radars detected approaching enemy aircraft and directed the Hellcats to intercept them. These destroyers had sustained heavy damage from the kamikazes, since they were usually the first ships to be sighted.

On May 28 my division took off on our first barrier patrol in cloudy and changing weather conditions. We were vectored by the ship's Combat Intelligence Center (CIC) to a point where a picket destroyer division CIC took control of us. We flew at five thousand feet, forty miles north of Okinawa, in broken cumulus clouds leaking light rain. They vectored us to a station at three thousand feet that was already occupied by a cloud. We flew around the clouds, staying as near the assigned locations as possible. From time to time, we saw the destroyer division that was directing us but stayed out of range of their hair-trigger gun crews. The flight continued for more than three hours. No kamikazes were flying our way that day.

We were flying in the same area where a former squadron member, Ensign Lerch, had flown to fame a few weeks earlier. Lerch had been in our fighter squadron until he broke his leg and was in the hospital when the squadron moved on. When he recovered, he transferred to a replacement squadron and found his way to combat before we did. Lerch looked and acted like an adolescent, and seemed to me too immature to meet the demands on us. He dropped out of our consciousness until a Navy newsletter reported that off Okinawa he had shot down five enemy planes in one flight, becoming an ace in one flight, a feat matched by only four other Americans in history,. But that didn't end it. On his second flight that day, he shot down two more, seven victories in one day! So much for evaluations based on appearances.

Near the end of our tour on station, rain and fog covered the task group, making it inadvisable to land on the *Ticonderoga*. Since it might be some hours before flying conditions improved, CIC directed us to land at Yontan Airfield on Okinawa to wait for orders. Finding and landing at Yontan presented no difficulties, and we parked our planes and checked out the place. I noticed what appeared to be scattered remains of aircraft along the parking area adjacent to the runway. On closer examination, they turned out to be the charred remains of engines, with propellers still attached. The engines were aligned in groups of four; there were perhaps as many as six groups. Surely something unusual had occurred here. An officer explained: In mid-May, during the landing of a group of aircraft, one plane landed wheels-up in the middle of the runway; eight or ten armed Japanese soldiers jumped from the craft and ran to a row of parked, four-engine aircraft. They scrambled onto them, opened the fueling ports, and inserted hand grenades. They then took pot-shots at the startled Marines and tried to escape into the surrounding countryside. Some succeeded. Their attack destroyed the aircraft. The fuel tanks were full of aviation gasoline and fed the fires, so the planes burned beyond recognition. A Betty (twin-engine Japanese bomber) had carried the Japanese suicide team.

I learned in 1989 that this account was incorrect. A flight of seven Japanese bombers loaded with troops had been sent out to attempt to crash land at Yontan. Night fighters and antiaircraft guns shot down six. One succeeded in landing. The troops from that one did all the damage. They destroyed forty aircraft, set gasoline storage tanks afire, and killed two Marines. Sixty-nine dead Japanese were found scattered on the airfield and in three bombers that crashed on the island. (Samuel Hynes, *Flights of Passage: Reflections of a World War II Aviator* [Boston: G. K. Hall, 1989].)

I also noticed that a few miles south of Yontan clouds of smoke and dust hung over the hills. I could hear the rumble of guns like distant thunder from the land battle. One can only imagine the chaos under that cloud. In contrast, after a somewhat amusing hour or two, we climbed back into our aircraft and flew to the *Ticonderoga,* where we could contemplate what might be served for chow that evening.

Hearing the guns booming on Okinawa caused me to reflect on the contrasting ways this war was being fought. Ours was a clean, gentlemanly, impersonal mode of fighting, while living in comfortable quarters being well cared for and well fed. When we went on a mission, we either returned and continued as before, or we were dead. No long suffering nor hospitalization, just a violent sudden end. An end believed by many to be the best, dying with your boots on, as the old aphorism goes. It had some appeal.

We were not only ordered to shoot down kamikazes before they reached Okinawa or the fleet, but we were to find and destroy them at their airfields before they could take off. That was a horse with a different colored tail. The enemy airfields nearest to Okinawa were near Kagoshima, on the south end of the Island of Kyūshū, a distance of more than three hundred miles, near the maximum range of the Hellcat with an auxiliary fuel tank. The distance was somewhat shortened when the task group moved northeast of Okinawa to launch and retrieve us.

The first strike of this kind remains a vivid memory for me. We took off in the predawn and rendezvoused, sixteen of us with the skipper in the lead. The skipper headed north toward Kagoshima Bay, a slot in the bottom of Kyūshū. At the head of the bay sat Ronchi Airfield, our target, known to be a launch point for kamikaze aircraft. En route we climbed to above ten thousand feet, changing course occasionally to avoid puffy clouds. We passed over two islands south of the bay, establishing that we were on course. They and the mountains around Kagoshima Bay were brilliantly green and peaceful looking. At the mouth of the bay we nosed down in a shallow descent, picking up speed to make us more difficult targets and reducing altitude for better viewing of the airfield. As we neared Ronchi airfield, puffs of black smoke appeared within a few hundred feet of us. I looked at it casually until I realized it was flak and it could kill me.

The skipper signaled to peel off for a strafing run. Until that time, most of my attention had been focused on maintaining position in formation. I didn't have a chance to look closely at the airfield, much less look long enough to find revetted and hidden aircraft. As I approached the edge of the field, my speed must have been around three hundred knots and my dive too steep to squeeze off more than a short burst into a dummy aircraft on the

Strafing runs were made against Ronchi Airfield, which was known to be a launch point for kamikaze aircraft.

runway. As I pulled out near level, I held the trigger down as a large thatched-roof structure came into my gunsight. Puffs of dust appeared as dozens of my .50-caliber bullets riddled the building. I leveled, and then climbed, with no targets in sight, toward the rendezvous point above a low volcano at the edge of the bay. The action lasted only a matter of seconds. Then we faced the long flight back to the *Ticonderoga*. They called it a "fighter sweep," but it more closely resembled a hit-and-run. Everyone

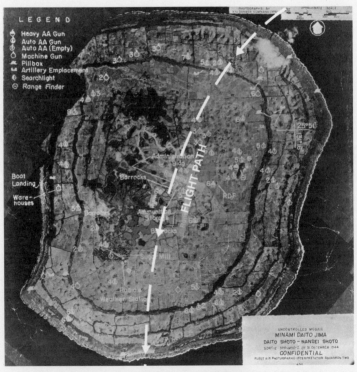

Napalm bombs were dropped on suspected antiaircraft installations, ground defenses, and alleged sources of strategic fiber materials thought to come from Minami Daitō Jima.

made it back aboard, though some claimed to be running on fumes. My flight time was 5.5 hours with fuel to spare.

I had inflicted zero damage, unless my slugs in the house and roof made it leak. No one did any better than that. The scary part of that strike was the possibility that we would run into fighter opposition. We would then be forced to operate the Hellcat at high-power settings, during which the engine gulped large amounts of fuel. Some planes, perhaps as many as half the flight, had barely enough fuel to land aboard the carrier; they would surely have been forced to make water landings. That would have made it a decisive Japanese victory.

We continued these actions until June 6, when the task force retired toward Leyte Gulf in the Philippine Islands. En route we made strikes in the Daitō Islands. My group dropped napalm bombs on suspected antiaircraft installations, ground defenses, and alleged sources of strategic fiber materials thought to come from Minami Daitō Jima. It seemed like just another realistic training exercise. I dropped napalm for the first time with no way of knowing whether that bomb inflicted any damage, but it made an enormous reddish yellow flame and a tall column of black smoke. I landed back aboard the *Ticonderoga* with a vague feeling of frustration that I had accomplished so little in exchange for so much risk. I stretched my imagination in vain to discover how those remote islands, cut off from Japan, could possibly be contributing anything to the Japanese war effort. I hoped I hadn't hurt anyone.

15

North to Japan with Task Group 38.3

At Leyte Gulf the task group broke apart. The bos'n whistled, "Now hear this! Now hear this! The anchoring detail lay forward to anchor. The anchoring detail lay forward to anchor." Soon the anchor plunged to the seafloor. The islands of Leyte and Samar, hilly and jungly, partially enclosed the roadstead. A half-hour boat ride took us to either island. The fleet would re-form there for a series of attacks on the Japanese home islands. Meanwhile, flight operations were suspended and the hours began to lengthen. Boredom set in.

In the late afternoon several times a week the bos'n's whistle would screech through the ship followed by "Now hear this! Now hear this! The movie detail lay forward on the hangar deck to rig for movies. The movie detail lay forward on the hangar deck to rig for movies." That provided a couple of hours of diversion. I was much impressed by the showing of *How Green Was My Valley* starring Donald Crisp. Occasional trips ashore to drink beer at the Macarata Officers' Club on Samar or snoop around the villages of Tacloban or Jinimog diverted us, but their abject poverty and war damage left little desire for a return trip. At Macarata, we drank beer with other squadron members around large picnic tables, talked of recent flights, and built pyramids out of emptied beer cans. Among the thousands of officers milling about, I occasionally saw someone I had known in training and swapped stories with them, a good reason to go. The boat ride back to the ship usually provided a laugh or two from the antics of the drunken officers. A man-overboard crisis would sometimes arise. But when on the ship, we had to call on our resources to keep occupied.

Some, like Mike, had an unlimited capacity to sleep, like a hibernating animal. He would eat an occasional meal or attend a squadron meeting, but would be back in the sack again a few minutes later, an effective way for him to make time pass. Basketball on the hangar deck or in the forward elevator killed time for me, but how much of that could you play in one day? I checked out the ship's library. The only book I could find containing any substance was entitled *The World's Ten Greatest Ideas*. It didn't take long to finish that one. Playing bridge became the ultimate time occupier for me. On the *Randolph*, months earlier, among a gathering of pilots, some had expressed an interest in learning bridge. As players became better informed about the game, some lost interest and others became more intrigued by it. Vic and I had become inseparable bridge partners, eager to challenge any other team. Our partnership continued aboard the *Ticonderoga*. During periods of minimal flying, we began playing in the wardroom after evening chow and continued through the night, until we ate breakfast and went to bed. This schedule had one serious disadvantage. During the day, chipping and painting in officer country was under way almost continuously. I sometimes thought, as I tried to sleep off a night of bridge, that the chipping was a conspiracy to deny me sleep.

At Leyte, we finally had a mail call. I received a letter from my brother-in-law Bob. Among the neutral family gossip in the letter, the statement that my uncle in New York was ill and in the hospital jumped out at me. This news didn't make any sense since I couldn't remember any uncle, much less one who lived in New York. Suddenly realizing that he had used our coded communications scheme, I dug out my copy of the list we had compiled and found New York listed as our name for the island of Tinian, in the Mariana Islands. I now had his location if the opportunity to use it presented itself.

The *Ticonderoga* left Leyte on July 1, headed north to Japan as part of Task Group 38.3, under Rear Admiral Bogan. Other carriers in the group were the *Essex,* the *Randolph,* and two light carriers, the *Monterrey* and *Bataan.* Two days out, a bearing on a propeller shaft burned out, requiring us to leave the task force with two escorting destroyers to put into the port of Apra, Guam. The repair parts had to be air freighted from Pennsylvania. Clearly, we would be at Guam for several days.

The Navy had constructed an officers' rest camp on Guam. We had been at sea now for three days, so we needed a rest. That place turned out to be a super Boy Scout camp with booze. It faced the ocean on a coral sand beach on the east side of the island, where a broad fringing coral reef uncovered at low tide. After a couple of days of horseshoe pitching, volleyball, reef roaming, and boozing, I began to look for transportation to Tinian to see Bob.

Tinian, then a base for hundreds of B-29s that were systematically destroying the cities of Japan, is 150 miles north of Guam. It turned out that two of my squadron mates were also anxious to go to Tinian, since they knew a couple of nurses stationed there. My buddy Sam, from the bomber squadron, also wanted to go, just to be going somewhere. A few phone calls and a trip to the local B-29 base resulted in our catching a ride to Tinian in an Army Air Forces transport. I had never seen such an enormous airfield. It had two parallel runways each several hundred feet wide and ten thousand feet long. The huge bombers were coming and going like angry bees at a disturbed hive.

It took several inquiries at the air base operations center to determine where a land-based naval air unit might be. We finally located it in a remote corner of the field. Sam and I scrounged a jeep ride to the site, where we found Bob. That ended the work-day for him. He took us to a primitive Chief's Club, short on facil-ities but long on beer. After a long afternoon and evening of beer drinking, I remember crouching on the ground with Sam and some of Bob's buddies, continuing to drink in the dark after the club closed. One of his buddies began to brag that he was the best man present. It sounded like a challenge, which it may have been, until I asked him on what he based his claim. With some hesita-tion he immodestly claimed that he could have five ejaculations on a single erection. No one could make a believable claim to match that one, so we conceded he was the best man and drank beer until it erased everything that happened after that.

Among the interesting tales of life on Tinian were those about Japanese who still hid out in the rough terrain near the base. From time to time, they sneaked onto the base to steal food and any-thing else not nailed down. Everyone on Tinian seemed to have a story about those Japanese holdouts, most unpleasant. Bob told us that at night, during the showing of movies in the outdoor the-ater, flashes of light that were believed to be Japanese soldiers lighting cigarettes while they, too, watched the movie could be seen on the high ground nearby.

We caught a ride back to Guam in a B-29 flown by a pilot prob-ably younger than any of us. I had never been in such a large air-plane. We were in a fish bowl called the cockpit, suspended in space looking over the pilot's shoulder, all the airplane behind us somewhere. He found Guam OK and made a miles-long straight-in approach. As he lost altitude, the nose of the plane swung slowly from side to side across the runway, the pilot's course an average of the swings. I lacked any feeling of how high we were off the runway. A prolonged mushy thump and an acceleration of the swinging as he rode the brakes announced our landing.

Within a few days the *Ticonderoga,* repaired and under way, rejoined Task Group 38.3, five hundred nautical miles southeast of

Tokyo. The task force was composed of four task groups each of which contained three to five aircraft carriers encircled by their supporting battleships, cruisers, and destroyers. The task groups were deployed twelve miles apart along a fleet axis that trended roughly parallel to Japan's coast. In our absence, it had made attacks on northern Japan and was prepared to hit the Inland Sea area. Refueling and replenishing continued through the twenty-third. Later that day, the task force began closing to within two hundred miles of the target area of attacks to begin the following morning.

At that stage of the war, the Japanese were saving their aircraft to repel the expected invasion of their homeland later in the year. Their strategy was to meet the invasion fleet with massive attacks by kamikaze aircraft that were being built and hidden near airfields in southern Japan. Our aircraft were meeting no airborne opposition nor were any strong attacks launched against the task force. Our counterstrategy was to destroy their aircraft on the ground and prepare to defend our invasion force with a wall of fighters.

Japanese airfields were linked to long taxi strips that meandered through the countryside. Off these strips were parking places for aircraft in revetments, circular earthen embankments higher than the aircraft. Camouflage netting covered most of them. They might contain an aircraft or they might not. Even good aerial photographs could not reduce that uncertainty by much. If you hit an aircraft, you would not know it since they were not fueled and no fire would result. They were fueled when ready for their last flight. We knew from experience that strafing such targets was a lost cause. We faced that prospect with misgivings.

16

We Regret to Inform You

On the afternoon of July 23 the skipper called a meeting to brief us on the next day's operations. We already knew what targets had been assigned to our squadron, but who would do what to which had not yet been revealed. From the excessive activity, chatter, wisecracking, and smoking before the briefing began, I sensed a high level of anxiety among the pilots. The skipper stood up. His aloof bearing silenced the noise and reminded me, "keep your distance, he's in charge here." I didn't know him personally but respected him as a talented man and officer.

Before turning the briefing over to our air intelligence officer, he methodically outlined the present tactical situation. He ended his short speech with "we will sweep the airfields in the Kure Area, shoot any aircraft out of the sky, and hunt and kill the bastards on the ground," a little bravado he tossed in to tweak our fighting spirits, out of character for him and inappropriate. No pep talk like that would stir me to long-odds heroic deeds. I knew what sweeps like that meant, and it depressed me. Just more wild, blind strafing of airfields, hoping to hit hidden kamikaze aircraft. Such flights just gave the Japanese antiaircraft gunners more practice.

Vic whispered to me, "Back in the shooting gallery as one of the ducks."

How much searching can you do, with no parked aircraft in sight, in a low-level run at 250 to 300 knots with enemy guns firing at you? Not much; you just blasted away and prayed they didn't blast you, then got the hell out of the range of their guns. There must be a better way.

The air intelligence officer charged my brain to well over capacity with photo intelligence reports, antiaircraft gun positions, radio communications frequencies, possible hiding places for aircraft, bail-out and ditching instructions, probable weather conditions, and diagrams of airfields. Then it was off to bed early to prepare for reveille before 0300 hours.

The first strike contained sixteen planes: four four-plane divisions led by the skipper. With a final briefing completed, we waited impatiently for the order "pilots, man your planes," given by the ship's air officer over the intercom system. When I trudged from the ready room and climbed to the flight deck I had antiblackout flight suit, helmet with goggles and earphones with dangling radio plug-in cable, parachute harness, inflatable life vest, .38-caliber pistol in a shoulder holster, ammunition belt, oxygen mask around my neck, backpack with survival gear, canteen of water, holstered knife, navigational plotting board, and gloves. Others also carried a rabbit's foot.

The flight deck, dark and washed by a cool brisk wind on our beam, rolled slowly as I threaded my way among the closely parked aircraft, their wings folded. I found my plane, with its maintenance captain standing on its wing; he helped me settle in the cockpit. I thanked him. "The plane's in good shape. Good luck!" he said; he gave me a pat on the shoulder and disappeared. I felt pangs of loneliness and thought, "will that be my last human contact?" I checked and rechecked flight details and waited for the bullhorn to announce "pilots, start your engines."

Planes were launched in the approximate order they would fly in the formation: the skipper went first, then his wingman, and so on. As tail-end-Charlie in the second four-plane division, led by Bill

Miller, I went eighth. During the launching, the new day's fingers were groping for the horizon. As the ship turned to port into the wind, she heeled noticeably to starboard. During the turn, the first planes were fired off the catapults. The turn completed, the ship righted herself, and the rest of the flight made deck-runs. I could see them as shadows darting up the deck, their engine exhausts aflame. When my turn came, deckmen with lighted wands signaled me to taxi clear of the other aircraft, where men spread and locked my wings. The deck officer gave me the rev up signal. I checked the magnetos at full power, nodded to him, and he signaled me to take off. I released the brakes and the plane lurched forward. I kept it on course with the rudder pedals. I couldn't see ahead until the tail came up and the bow rushed toward me. I eased back on the stick, felt the plane lighten and leave the deck. I pulled in the wheels and flaps.

The Hellcat ahead of me had disappeared into the predawn gloom, so I made for the rendezvous point and climbed to the correct altitude. By now, dawn gripped the horizon. I could see only one plane circling what I believed to be our rendezvous point. Where were the other six planes that took off ahead of me? When I joined up I could see the skipper, his angular head jerking from side to side looking for the other planes as he flew in tight circles that I imagined corresponded to twists in his gut. To fly wing on him bumped up my stress level a notch.

After what seemed to me an eternity of this fuel-consuming circling, but was actually only ten minutes or so, six planes found us. We were still short eight planes. What would the skipper do? He broke radio silence, contacted the rest of the flight, and ordered them to rendezvous at Angels 12 at Point Ash, a code name for the nearest point of land. He signaled that we were to remain in our present flying positions rather than try to unscramble the formation. That meant I would continue to fly on his wing, an honor I'd have been pleased to yield to anyone. This muddled rendezvous and the extra fuel it consumed was a bad start on our maximum-range flight.

Within an hour we sighted land through breaks in the clouds, and our eight missing planes joined up. We flew up Bungo Suido, an entrance to the Inland Sea, with the west coast of Shikoku in sight on our right, a green, mountainous island with terraced rice paddies far up the mountains where they gave way to forests that were partly obscured by clouds. The skipper led us below a lowering ceiling to maintain visual contact with the ground, along the coast northeast toward our first target, Matsuyama West Airfield, near the shore. Vertical air photos had shown many aircraft there in revetments. We found the field, but from our low-angle approach, it looked nothing like the air photos. We made a low-level strafing attack in which I could not pick out a meaningful target in the few seconds between peeling out of formation and getting within firing range. I couldn't see a revetment, much less an airplane in it. To avoid power lines along the edge of the field, I pulled up sharply. It angered me to be exposed to ground fire with so little chance of inflicting significant damage.

We gained altitude and joined up over water where two oil tankers steamed north in the Inland Sea. The skipper signaled us to attack the nearest tanker. These targets would be worth the risk. We would fire rockets at them. I moved into position a hundred feet abeam and starboard of the skipper and began our attack, firing all six .50-caliber machine guns in bursts to suppress any defensive fire the ship might offer. Astonished, I saw the skipper fire a pair of rockets at long range. They arced gracefully through the air and hit the water hundreds of yards short of the target. With that faulty rocket shot in mind, I pushed my attack with machine guns to point-blank range before I fired a pair of rockets, almost an unintentional kamikaze attack. I can still call up the image of the tanker's mast in my windshield, the sound of my exploding rockets, and the sight of the shrapnel they spewed up around me.

That part of the strike rated as a satisfying, unqualified success. The rockets had the impact of 5-inch artillery shells, and the planes that followed also inflicted enormous damage to the ships. We left them burning and sinking. I briefly visualized the chaos on the ships, dead and wounded men, others struggling out of flooding engine rooms only to face a wall of burning oil. But those thoughts were pushed from my mind by the need to fly the airplane and join up on the skipper. The flight deteriorated rapidly after that.

We made a feint toward Iwakuni Air Base while our photo plane took pictures. Then the skipper, without apparent reason, led us within the air defense zone of the Kure Naval Base, from which black puffs of flak appeared menacingly close. Some of us zigzagged out of the area, but he held a steady course. We headed

An unexpected change in flight plan took Lieutenant Vernon's bombing-fighting group into the air defense zone of the Kure Naval Base.

for our next target, Niihama Airfield on the north shore of
Shikoku. En route someone discovered two four-engine flying
boats anchored in a cove. The skipper, after some hesitation,
directed the second two divisions to attack them while we flew
cover. The boats were left sinking in shallow water.

Gray and foreboding overcast skies blanketed Niihama. They
forced us to start our strafing run below three thousand feet, in a
sweeping left turn. I thought, "here we go again, ducks in a shooting gallery." I flew on the skipper's right. The other two planes in
the division moved to our right on the outside of the turn. We

En route to Niihama Airfield, Lieutenant Vernon's group struck
Matsuyama West Airfield.

straightened our course in a seaward direction and began firing at anything in our sight, which was not much. In a few seconds, we skimmed the water at high speed. Several ominous puffs of dark debris appeared around the tail section of the skipper's plane. I glanced away for an instant and then back to him. A stupefying scene unfolded.

The skipper's canopy opened, he stood up, his parachute streamed out and jerked him clear of the plane. The Hellcat hit the water with the skipper a few feet to the right of it. His parachute didn't blossom to check his fall; he plunged feet first into the murky, shallow water and disappeared. The shroud of his parachute floated on the surface; its lines extended downward, fading from sight into his dark watery grave, next to the partly submerged, drowning Hellcat. As my mind played and replayed that stunning scene, my training and instincts flew the airplane. I banked to the left and, with two others, circled the wreck. It took several minutes for the finality of his death to sink in and to remember that the Japanese were still shooting at us from the airfield. When it did, we responded to Bill Miller's insistent call "Join-up! Join-up! Join-up!"

I saw the rest of our group a mile to the west. I headed toward them to begin the long, sad flight to the *Ticonderoga*. It relieved me that although a key man fell, another took command. We would carry on as we had in the past, when Dick and Leon and Art and Joe and Joey and others had fallen. I flew, dazed and unbelieving, during the return flight. The skipper always had appeared to me an aloof, invincible leader who would always lead and be the last to fall. Those feelings about him heightened the impact of his death on me. The shock of seeing the skipper crash is still a vivid image that often returns to me.

We retreated through Bungo Suido to the "safety" of the open sea. Picket destroyers fifty miles offshore gave us an updated course to the task force, yet another hundred miles away. We flew low over the sea through light rain, below a somber, low overcast that matched my spirits. I saw other planes through the drizzle in loose formation skimming the water, like weary migrating ducks seeking a safe place to land.

I thought about my gas supply. It was going to be close, despite starving the engine throughout the flight. Others reported their fuel perilously low; Bateman ditched near a destroyer and Morey landed on another carrier. I felt drained of energy like my reserve fuel tank, whose gauge showed near empty. Bill found the task force and our carrier, and led us into the landing pattern. With great effort, I blotted from my mind the dead skipper and the fuel

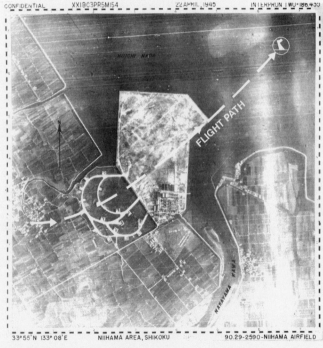

Commander Porter Maxwell's plane was shot down over the water near Niihama Airfield; the skipper did not survive the crash.

tank, whose gauge now showed empty but quivered a little, indicating that some gasoline remained, and focused my attention on flying. I landed aboard safely, more than five hours after takeoff.

As the only pilot who saw the skipper crash, I had to repeat my story many times, beginning with the debriefing to the air intelligence officer, executive officer, and others in the squadron, and ultimately to the air group commander, who had to report the circumstances of his death to the skipper's wife. He asked several penetrating questions to be absolutely certain that the skipper had died in the crash and was not just missing in action, a distinction of great importance to his family. There was no doubt in my mind nor in the minds of the two other pilots who had circled the wreck. He was dead.

Writing such letters was a painful experience for the commander. The widow would have received through official channels a telegram: "We regret to inform you that your husband . . ." with no specifics. The details in the commander's letter would be a second shock to the wife and family, and a delayed sorrow for his newborn when old enough to grasp the truth. I envisioned photographs of the skipper hung in some honored niche in their shattered household, a superficial image of a deep, talented, and brave man. I also thought of the quirkiness of fate, that the bullets that downed him had missed me, flying only yards away from him.

The unofficial comments among the pilots had a different tone from the official debriefings. I wondered why the skipper had fired his rockets at the tanker at such long range that they hit far off the target. Several men could not understand why he led us at low altitude needlessly through a known heavy concentration of anti-aircraft batteries in the Kure area and why he took no evasive actions when flak burst thick among us. Why did he deviate from the strike plan? He led us far from the planned route, making it doubtful that we would have enough fuel to return to the carrier. Why was he so slow to respond to the sighting of the two seaplanes? Why didn't he take evasive action after the strafing run at

Niihama? There may have been reasonable answers to those questions, but they died with him. And who would have asked them had he lived? Not I.

I alerted the plane captain that there might be damage to the Hellcat I had flown. Together, we examined the bottom surfaces of wings and fuselage where we counted more than half a dozen holes. The strike schedule for that afternoon and the following morning listed my name. But I must have appeared drained and shaken by that morning's experience; at least the flight surgeon thought so. After debriefing me, he gave me a couple of shots of medicinal whiskey, chatted with me for a few minutes, and had me removed from the second strike of the day.

With the skipper gone, LCDR Walter Haas became the commanding officer of the squadron. The transition of command was smooth and, at least to us, the junior officers, hardly noticeable. The Navy system worked. The only difference was that now, instead of the stern, aloof Commander Porter Maxwell, we had a relaxed leader who, when addressing us in the ready room, began with, "Well, gents . . ." I felt I barely knew this quiet man. I hoped to know him better as time passed.

The same day the skipper died, the bomber squadron had sent out all fourteen of its operational planes to attack the battleship *Hyuga*, at anchor near the naval base at Kure. The *Hyuga* and nearby ships and islands were loaded with antiaircraft batteries. We expected heavy losses. My buddy Sam flew that strike, which began ominously. The first bomber went off the bow into the water and the pilot drowned. That left thirteen planes to make the attack. Several hours later, when the bos'n's whistle sounded "Now hear this! Now hear this! The smoking lamp is out on the main deck level and above while landing aircraft," I climbed to the flight deck thinking that the bombers had returned from the strike. We were in squally weather, with low clouds and scattered rain. Six bombers straggled into the traffic pattern. One plane fouled the deck by jumping the barrier and crashing on the plane

F6F Hellcat ready to begin a deck launch.
U.S. Naval Institute

that had landed ahead of it. The deck was cleared by pushing that plane over the side. During the clearing, all other landing craft were waved off. Eventually, four came aboard safely, the fifth ditched, and a destroyer rescued the men.

Sam did not land. I feared the worst. After several anxious hours, good news arrived. He had landed safely on another carrier.

A special friend, Eppa Vaughn, did not return from that flight. He'd made a steep dive on the *Hyuga* but didn't pull out. He plunged into the water close to the *Hyuga* and disappeared in a towering geyser. He had done his part in sinking that huge ship. In that strike, the bomber squadron was reduced to five planes from fifteen. But all five flew on the second strike of the day.

The next day, strikes were launched against other targets on the Inland Sea. In a predawn launch of sixteen planes, we aimed at Kure Naval Air Station and Hiro seaplane base. At that time of year, a more or less continuous front of clouds lies along the east coast of Japan. At the task force, the ceiling was broken at two thousand feet, with scattered light rain. Not wanting to approach the coast at low altitude under those conditions, we climbed above the clouds at launch. Ahead, we could see that the cloud tops were still higher. We continued to climb. At sixteen thousand feet, we were still skimming the clouds, clawing toward the top.

We began hearing repeated plaintive calls, "Tony, I can't keep up. Wait for me." Fred Woods, the last man in the formation, had trouble. We continued past seventeen thousand feet. The call came again, then silence. Several minutes later, we received a weaker transmission from Fred in a quavering voice. "I'm below the clouds, request instructions." Our flight leader replied, "Return to home plate."

We finally topped the cloud bank above eighteen thousand feet. We could see Japan ahead in the clear. As we began losing altitude and gaining speed over Shikoku, a large flight of planes, perhaps as many as fifty, appeared at four o'clock, at our altitude. Momentarily startled, I saw they were P-51s that had flown up from Iwo Jima. They recognized us as friendlies and slanted off to the north, toward Osaka. We strafed the airfields as ordered, with the usual uncertain results, and returned to the *Ticonderoga* below the overcast. We suffered no losses.

Happily, we found Fred safely aboard and heard his hair-raising story. He had lagged below the rest of the flight, had scraped off into a cloud, lost control, and had fallen into a spin. He had spun down through the gloomy cloud for fourteen thousand feet before he fell out of its bottom at two thousand feet, like awakening from a bad dream, and recovered control at the wave tops.

That evening the fleet moved offshore to resupply. For a few days we could relax.

17

Typhoon Season

On the twenty-sixth and twenty-seventh of July, the task force began refueling and replenishing five hundred miles southeast of Shikoku. The bos'n squealed, "Now hear this! Now hear this! The smoking lamp is out on the main deck level and above while refueling. The smoking lamp is out on the main deck level and above while refueling." With elegant precision, a tanker moved in one hundred feet abeam of us on a parallel course and deployed refueling hoses. A destroyer fell in on the opposite side of the tanker and began to take fuel also. Within a few hours, our tanks were filled and the refueling rigging cast off. A reefer appeared out of nowhere, took the tanker's position, and deployed lines to transfer stores, equipment, and replacement pilots. Complex logistical planning was required to deliver these materials to us. Our problems seemed simple and straightforward by comparison. We would strike targets on the Inland Sea beginning on the twenty-eighth of July.

Meanwhile, we received a briefing for a future strike on shipping and harbor facilities in, of all places, Pusan, Korea. That would mean flying across the Inland Sea, southern Honshū, the

VBF 87 ready room aboard the *Ticonderoga,* August 1945, off the coast
of Japan. Lieutenant Vernon is against bulkhead (*far left, below white
cloth*). The skipper, Commander Haas, is second from right in row
behind desk.

fifty-mile-wide Korean Strait, and returning. In case of an emergency, we could land at Vladivostok! I could scarcely believe such
a strike would be considered. It would essentially be a one-way
mission, given the known range of the Hellcat. Vic said, "It's some
admiral's wet dream." That plan was dead on arrival as far as we
were concerned. Officially, it died a silent, well-deserved, and
unregretted death.

On the twenty-eighth, more strikes hit the Inland Sea area, but
I flew a combat air patrol that day, five hours of formation flying
over and near the fleet. CIC assigned an altitude and a position to
hold, from which we could be vectored toward any unidentified
aircraft, called a bogie. It was dull, tedious flying in loose formation. By now, formation flying had become almost instinctive and
effortless. We had much time on our hands, flying in circles with
nothing to do but stay awake and listen for instructions from CIC.

On some of these flights, I wrote letters. I used my plotting board as a writing surface, flew with the stick in my left hand, and wrote with my right, occasionally stopping to adjust the throttle. I had now logged dozens of hours on stupefying combat air patrols with never a sniff of an enemy aircraft. Other pilots had had similar experiences.

That day, I lost another friend from the bomber squadron, Raymond Porter. He flew to attack the heavy cruiser *Tone* in the Kure area, like the *Hyuga* heavily defended by AA batteries on nearby islands. Porter completed his diving attack but showed up at the rendezvous point with his engine belching smoke. He headed out along the retirement course but had to ditch in the Inland Sea. He and his aircrewman survived, broke out their life raft, and drifted hopefully in that unfriendly sea. Several fighters from our squadron circled over them, prepared to fight off any enemy air or surface craft. They tried desperately to call in a PBY rescue seaplane but failed. Eventually, with gasoline running low, they had to say a sad good-bye to them with a final low pass, rocking their wings, and headed south toward the task force. We were all hopeful, even certain, that they would be picked up by the enemy surface craft that were in the area. Better to be a prisoner of war than dead by drowning, I thought.

Porter and Brisette, his aircrewman, were not returned as prisoners of war. The U.S. government kept their fate secret for thirty years. It finally came out, as we had expected, that they had been captured, eventually being confined in a prison called Hiroshima Castle, along with eight Army Air Forces personnel. On August sixth the atomic bomb exploded over Hiroshima. All died in the blast or from radiation sickness. Drowning at sea would have been a kinder fate.

Typhoon season had arrived in the South China Sea and western Pacific off southern Japan, and one approached our operating area. Each task group commander was given discretion to maneuver to avoid the storm. Our commander, Rear Admiral Bogan, elected to steer south three hundred miles. Flight operations were canceled; planes moved to the hangar deck; and the ship buttoned up. Seas, pushed by winds over sixty knots, built to thirty feet and more. Clouds filled with rain and salty spray hugged the water, lowering the visibility to less than a mile. The *Ticonderoga* wallowed doggedly through the raging sea. Pitching and rolling for two days and a night, she cried like a keening squaw, metal against metal as she flexed. Cascading green water and foam intermittently washed the flight deck, ordinarily fifty feet above the sea.

At night I lay in my bunk, rolling from side to side, alternately shoved against the cold metal of the bulkhead and the bunk rail. Sleep was elusive. I was trapped in a steel box from which it would be difficult to escape. My fate rested in the hands of the men who had built the ship and those who operated her. If she foundered in this storm, the chance of my surviving was one in several hundred. I tried not to worry about that over which I had no control. But those thoughts kept coming back to me as I was randomly pressed hard against the mattress as the ship climbed a wave, and then felt weightless when she plunged into a trough, while listening to the plaintive cries of the struggling ship, a lullaby for the doomed.

Admiral Bogan's course for the task group proved fortunate. The eye of the typhoon passed west and north of us. Other task groups were not as fortunate, suffering heavy losses of ships and men. It took several days following the storm to reassemble the task force and steam to northern Japan, which we began striking on August 9.

During a break in the action, we took aboard replacement pilots and aircraft, flown to us from jeep carriers, part of the logistical support group of the task force. After one strike, a replacement pilot, Butcher, was sent on his first CAP. Butcher described that experience in a squadron publication, "September Song II."

After noon chow I heard my name called with orders to report to the ready room. When I got there Jim Mantis explained that there had been heavy incursions of kamikazes and that extra CAP was needed so he volunteered us. (I didn't know Lieutenants ever volunteered for anything.) So we deck launched (a civilized method of departing the ship) at about 1500 hours, as I recall it.

Jim had said, "You are doing OK, Butch, so I'll take back my regular wing man 'Sugar' and you go back and fly wing on Bill." Since then I've read several different scenarios in that but, anyway, I flew on Bill who said, "Just stay on my wing—if I want you to weave, I'll let you know!"

First we went to 25,000 feet and then down to 15,000 then to 10,000 vectoring out to an incoming kamikaze. We spotted him out of a left turn to intercept. Right there Bill did a shrewd thing by sliding under Jim and Sugar to the inside of the turn so I slid under him, thinking "hot damn, this puts me on the inside of the turn—I'll get first crack at this baby." Well, about that time Bill and Sugar and Jim all started to fly around me on the outside of the turn. I thought, "What's the matter with this scow I'm flying?" I had it "fire-walled" and couldn't keep up. I looked down and I was still in hi-blower using up about 150 horsepower that they weren't.

As I pulled off the supercharger Bill started to shoot. So did Jim and Sugar. Bill's shell casings started pouring out of the discharge chutes and I thought, "Judas Priest, I'm going to get killed by Bill's empties!"

Well, it was just like the best movie of shooting down the enemy you ever saw. First the left wheel fell out of the wheel well and then it started shedding parts and pieces. Just about the time I wondered if I would make it flying through all the junk in the air a huge red ball of fire showed up as it exploded and threw more pieces in our way.

Somehow we all made it through. Bill got credit for the kill. I can't say for sure who did it—but—I know who didn't—ME! I was so busy trying to catch up and get out of the way of flying shell cases and airplane parts that I didn't get him in my sights that I can remember it.

They shifted us to the *Monterrey* fighter director and he sent us to 10,000. Jim and Sugar had pickeled off their belly tanks for the first attack but I was more scared of running out of fuel than anything else so I still had mine and Bill had his, too.

Jim had explained that they had special procedures in his division to accommodate the fact that he really couldn't see all that well (he had memorized the eye chart). SOP would be that if Jim missed the "tally-ho," whoever made it would lead the attack. This usually meant that Sugar did it—he could REALLY see!

Anyway, the weather was lousy—lots of clouds—so when the FDO gave us a target and a vector, Jim called Bill and said "go to formation X-ray." (I wondered what the heck that was.) It appeared Bill couldn't hear Jim so I told him that, and he said, "OK—you go." It was a little embarrassing but I asked him what I was to do and he explained he wanted one section above the clouds and one below. For him, he was pretty emphatic about it, so I broke off and let down below the clouds. We were in a right hand turn but as soon as I broke out I saw the "bandit" at my nine o'clock position, tally-hoed and turned to chase him.

I looked back and saw the rest of the division breaking out below the clouds which firmed my resolve. I "fire-walled" it. I knew that the F6 was faster than the "Judy" I was chasing. It was! The Japanese pilot knew I was there and shut off all the power. The next thing I knew I was not only catching him but was in real danger of flying right on by him. (I had thought those guys were supposed to be dumb!) I didn't care to find out if he could shoot so I shut everything down—threw out the gear, and dropped the flaps. Given that I was way over-speed for that kind of stuff I have had plenty of time to thank God and Grumman that the airplane hung together. Even at that, I didn't get slowed down until I was flying close (REALLY close) wing on this guy and we were looking at each other eye-to-eye.

Well, I got the airplane cleaned up just about the time he turned into me. I guess he thought that if he couldn't get a carrier he would at least try for me. (He got one more notch of respect from me.)

I booted the thing around until I got on his tail and was able to open fire. I was looking for the kind of fireworks display we had had earlier but nothing happened. I was firing short bursts and figured it wasn't working so I held the trigger down and "walked" the tracers in. As it turned out, he had been taking hits because the next thing that happened was he flew into the ocean just in time to alert me that I was in serious danger of following him in. I've always thought the splash went about as high as my wing tip but that may be a bit graphic.

Butcher had done what we had all hoped to do, see and shoot down an enemy aircraft, on his first CAP! It didn't seem fair. There's no substitute for having the luck to be in the right place at the right time.

After a day of strikes against the Kōbe-Nagoya area, the task force retired again for refueling and replenishing. For some reason, probably political and diplomatic, further attacks were not made for a week.

18

A Waste of Men in a
War Already Won

That week, a B-29 dropped an atomic bomb on Hiroshima. None of us had ever heard of an atomic bomb, but reports of its devastating effects made us feel certain that the war would be over within hours. It seemed sufficient reason to celebrate. High-class booze that had been jealously guarded for months surfaced in our rooms; celebrations continued into the early hours of the morning. That same morning, we were dismayed to learn that flight operations would proceed with our pinprick attacks. On the schedule were combat air patrols and strikes against targets in northern Honshū and Hokkaido.

By this time, a new bomb fuse had been supplied to us called the "proximity" fuse. It sensed its distance to any large object, like the earth and, we believed, an airplane. When armed it would ignite the bomb at a set distance from an object. This device in a fragmentation bomb had the potential of saturating a considerable ground area with shrapnel when exploded a hundred feet or more above the ground, like a shotgun blast. To me, it seemed a more effective weapon against hidden aircraft than blind strafing and, at least of equal importance, safer for the pilot to deliver from a dive with a pullout above fifteen hundred feet, than strafing at low altitude. But we also had reservations about them. If by chance a bomb became armed while still on the aircraft, the aircraft was the most proximal object.

I dropped two of those bombs in strikes on airfields in northern Honshū. On the first strike, against Misawa Airfield, I released my bomb from a steep dive. As I pulled out at fifteen hundred feet, a bomb exploded at my altitude several hundred feet away. I reported this unusual happening when debriefed. Others had seen the same explosion. Apparently, the proximity fuse had malfunctioned, suggesting to us that they were unreliable and dangerous. After the war I learned that eight Corsair fighters exploded, one by one, while carrying those bombs. Vic said, "An explosion like that could ruin your whole day."

We lost two pilots on the second day of the strikes on northern Honshū, a tragic waste of men in a war already won. While attacking shipping in Aomori Bay, Pete, a senior lieutenant, took an antiaircraft hit and had to bail out. He landed in the bay near shore. His flying mates followed him down, but could find only his parachute floating on the water. A seaplane sent to search for him found nothing. Later that day, after attacking Ominato Naval Base, Bill, another lieutenant, caught heavy flak but stayed aloft until he made a water landing several miles offshore. Pilots who escorted him until he landed saw him climb from the cockpit onto the wing and then wave as the plane began to sink. Strangely, he went under with the plane, leaving not a trace.

The second atomic bomb had been dropped. The Soviet Union had entered the war against Japan, and Japan had accepted the Allied Potsdam ultimatum. We were all certain that the war was over. We could see no reason for continuing to risk our precious skins by striking more targets in Japan. But that sentiment did not coincide with those of the men who were running the war. We would make another series of strikes two days later, August 13, against targets in the Tokyo area.

On the morning of August 13, 1945, off Tokyo, I flew an uneventful five-hour combat air patrol over the task force. In the afternoon, Al Cassidy and I were given a submarine combat air patrol. We were to provide protection to a rescue submarine stationed off Irō-Zaki, a cape on the southwesterly approach to Sagami and Tokyo Bays. When we arrived on station, we contacted the submarine that had surfaced so that any aircraft in trouble could land near it. We orbited the cape at 3,000 feet for an hour or so, staying very alert. That became boring. Couldn't we do some damage to the enemy instead of this? The only likely looking target was a lighthouse. Our adolescent instincts for vandalism surfaced. We would strafe the lighthouse. It stood 50 to 100 feet high on a rocky point. We made several strafing passes at it, knocking out the 360-degree light window and perforating adjacent buildings. There was no sign of life, understandably; people stayed under cover while being strafed.

The submarine, a mile or so offshore, wanting to get in on the fun, called us to say they would fire a few practice rounds at the lighthouse with their deck gun. Would we spot their hits for them? We agreed. Their accuracy surprised me. Their first shot was long by 100 feet; with our calls they began to strike closer, but they didn't hit it. That suited us, because we wanted to take full credit for disabling half a lighthouse each. We felt that would be a unique distinction, perhaps even meriting a decoration of some kind. Perhaps we could count it as a strike on enemy positions toward a Distinguished Flying Cross. No enemy planes or crippled aircraft came our way. We departed for the *Ticonderoga*. Looking back, I had my last view of Japan while it was still in a state of war.

On August 15 some 200 miles off the coast, we launched another series of strikes against the Tokyo area. I flew in one of the usual defensive combat air patrols at 10,000 feet over picket destroyers. After orbiting at that altitude for an hour, we received instructions from our fighter direction center, Ginger Base, to go to 15,000 feet on vector so-and-so, almost immediately followed by directions to go to 20,000 feet and look for a bogie. Maybe this would be my first chance to have a shot at an airborne enemy aircraft. At 20,000 feet, we were directed to go to 25,000 feet and "keep climbing on the same vector and keep your eyes peeled." They still had the bogie on their radarscope. At 26,000 feet in hazy visibility, we strained onward and upward with no bogie in sight.

Communications from Ginger Base stopped for several minutes. Still no bogie. Then came the communication "Ginger One Niner, this is Ginger Base, over."

Bill Miller answered, "This is One Niner, over."

"One Niner, this is Ginger Base. Discontinue all offensive actions against enemy forces. Do not attack enemy forces, but if threatened, shoot them down in a friendly manner. A cease-fire has been declared."

"This is Ginger One Niner, affirmative, in a friendly manner, out."

And so the war ended, as I sucked oxygen at 26,000 feet chasing a bogie we couldn't see. We believed that the bogie we futilely chased was a stripped-down, twin-engine Betty bomber equipped for swift, high-altitude reconnaissance to determine the location of our task force. We heard other pilots on our frequency acknowledge the good news in formal jargon, as we had, and some yelps of irreverent pleasure from unidentified pilots unable to suppress their exhilaration. My reaction was reverential.

Our planes returned from the strikes without further losses, having dropped the last bombs of the war on Japan. The task force opened the distance between itself and the coast and maintained a defensive posture in the event some fanatical diehard tried another kamikaze attack. We remained in that condition until August 22, when we launched yet another superfluous flight. On this one, the usual radio silence did not prevail. The war was won;

peace was ours. But it happened that the day was made gloomy by scattered rainsqualls, like black pillars supporting a low, gray ceiling. Although somewhat apprehensive of the hazards these dramatic conditions suggested, I sank into mechanically flying in formation and musing. We would soon be headed home, an event that evoked happy and tender thoughts. This ocean was ours, below us floated the greatest fleet in history.

In the tradition of the victorious military, a parade of air power was in progress. The aircraft carriers of the U.S. Third Fleet had spewed out more than fifteen hundred aircraft, which formed a sinuous, amorphous organism. Releasing myself briefly from the hypnotic influence of holding my place in formation, I could see obliquely on my left the main body of the flight stacked from the overcast to the sea and extending for miles along its course. Like an enormous serpent, it moved relentlessly through an irregular colonnade of black pillars of rain. I felt a wave of pride to be part of that dazzling display of victorious power and skill.

Now, small shafts of sunlight squeezed through the clouds, adding a touch of well-being to an otherwise somber scene. Suddenly, from thoughts like these, I felt apprehension as I observed with alarm the closeness of the other airplanes and the irregularity of the course being flown. Three years of flying had made me alert to approaching danger. I saw that we were now flying along the right flank of the massed formation, which was attempting to fly a midcourse between rainsqualls. If the flight were too wide to squeeze between the squalls, what would we on the flanks do? Any action would be constrained by the clouds above, the sea below, and the airplanes on all sides. These thoughts could not have been unique among the hundreds of fliers present.

Ahead, a black squall appeared, a misty mass, perhaps ten miles off, silently announcing a coming crisis. We were hurtling down a threatening, constricting corridor, roofed by dense clouds, floored by turbulent water, walled by massed aircraft, into an ominous black curtain. As we neared, the squall became sharply defined and blacker, clearly a place to avoid. If we were forced to enter it and visual contact was lost, I would be one of dozens of planes flying blindly in pelting rain, expecting a collision at any instant.

The planes ahead continued unswervingly toward the squall. I waited tensely for the leaders to do something. If they did not, what should I do, follow them sheeplike into the squall? Suddenly the lead airplanes began a steep turn to starboard. We reversed course, narrowly avoiding the planes on our flank, because they abruptly sheered away. Our closely packed squadron of thirty-six airplanes swept through the turn, away from certain peril and into a yet more frightening path, which seemed to guarantee catastrophe. Before us now appeared a squadron of Corsair fighters in tight formation, winging straight at us; the blur of their whirling, glinting propellers projected a menacing message. We were now closing on a collision course at the rate of six miles per minute.

The Corsairs were flying in divisions of four planes, like we were, all within a division flying at near the same level. Other divisions were flying stepped down tens of feet below the lead division and a short distance to either side. We both presented a front several hundred feet wide and deep. We were five hundred feet above the sea and five seconds from a collision. Within two seconds, it was clear to me that no abrupt evasive maneuver by me was possible without aggravating our already grave situation. We were nose to nose with four Corsairs. Our only hope was to fly between the divisions, above or below the one on our nose, like cards being shuffled. Did the Corsair pilots think as I did? Did Bill Miller? Suppose we headed for a narrow gap in their formation and they did the same toward one of ours? Second number three ticked by, still no adjustment by Bill. Instinctively, we all tucked in close to him, like frightened chicks to a hen, to make us as compact as possible. A vision of an eight-plane head-on collision flashed through my mind. My fate was in others' hands. I could only hold steady and wait. I thought, "if Bill is as steady and brave a man as I believe him to be, he will make a move to save us." At second number four, Bill nosed his plane down a few feet; we clung to him.

He headed under the nearest Corsairs. We had a chance, if they stayed their course! The Corsairs continued flying straight and level. In a breathtaking blur we plunged under them and they were gone, the turbulence of their passing jostling us. The air ahead was clear and our division was safe; I could breathe again. Below us, two levels of Corsairs, one group at wave-top, clawed into a steep right turn for they too had to avoid the rainsquall. I glimpsed a splash on the white-capped sea. Was it a plane down or a breaking wave? No time to look. Above us, several levels of Hellcats and Corsairs zigzagged crazily to avoid each other and the clouds above. Bill made a shallow climbing right turn to rejoin our scattered squadron. That brave man looked back and

VBF 87 aboard the USS *Ticonderoga*, September 1945. Lieutenant Vernon is third row from back, second from right. Commander Haas, the skipper, is center of second row from bottom.

The VBF 87 squadron patch.

passed his left hand over his brow in a classic, sweat-wiping motion and cast his face and eyes heavenward with understated eloquence.

That flight became known as "the Group Grope to End All Group Gropes." It was a source of anger, resentment, and emphatic criticism among pilots. Why in hell had Admiral Halsey scheduled such a dangerous flight under those weather conditions? We thought it was a stupid, self-serving decision. No one was killed, but we can't thank Halsey for that. Vic said, "It was just another admiral's wet dream, probably wanting to establish a new world record for numbers of carrier-launched aircraft flying in formation."

August 25 found our part of the task force east of Kyūshū. We provided cover for destroyers carrying occupational forces to Tokyo and patrolled airfields in the Inland Sea to check Japanese compliance with the terms of the cease-fire. They were not to fly any aircraft; those they had were to be parked in the open on the airfields. The naval vessels were to be removed from camouflage and anchored in an open roadstead.

Those flights were invitations to flat-hatting around the airfields we had attacked and from which we had dodged flak. They

Lieutenant Vernon in flight gear, 1944.

satisfied some of our curiosity about details of the countryside and culture that were easily overlooked in attack runs at three hundred knots. By far, the most impressive sight was Hiroshima. I had passed it during an attack in July, noting that it appeared to be an orderly city. Now the only sign that it had once been a city was a network of streets that were cleared of debris and a few damaged concrete structures. Hiroshima was partly surrounded by steep hills once covered by lush green vegetation. Now they were brown, an isolated, instant, atomic-autumn scene.

We wondered what would become of us and when, now that the war was over. The Navy surprised us by announcing a demobilization plan, a simple point system based on years of service, combat experience, medals, dependents, and so on. That made most of our senior officers eligible for immediate discharge. On August 30 some took the first opportunity to leave the *Ticonderoga* for a homeward-bound ship. They transferred at sea.

During the early morning of September 6 the *Ticonderoga* steamed into Tokyo Bay to join hundreds of ships already there.

The bos'n's whistle shrilled through the ship, "Now hear this! Now hear this! The anchoring detail lay forward to anchor. The anchoring detail lay forward to anchor."

When the *Ticonderoga* stopped dead in the water off Yokohama, the anchor chain thundered down the hawse pipe, and the anchor plunged into the murky water. She had been on the move, out of sight of land, since July 19 when we had left Guam, fifty days earlier.

19

An Uncertain Future

Japan now lay only a short boat ride away. From the flight deck of the *Ticonderoga,* I could see the low skyline of Yokohama and Tokyo nearby, dimly far up the bay. We were all eager to go ashore. Within a day of anchoring, a schedule of shore boats was set up to carry crewmembers for day-visits to Yokohama. Those who had the time and wanted to visit Tokyo could ride a train from Yokohama. Some squadron members were permitted to go ashore each day. My turn came shortly before we were to depart for Hawaii; by then I had little desire to see Yokohama. I had heard from others what to expect, and it didn't sound inviting.

I had much time to think while waiting day after day on the anchored, resting ship. The goals of training, flying, surviving, combat, winning the war had been attained. What was left? It gave me a vaguely empty feeling. My thoughts turned from the war that was no more toward the future. What should my future goals be? Could I create any goals that would be as inspiring as the ones that were forced on me by the war? It didn't seem likely. Was this the culmination of my life's effort, as it had been for those men we had lost, or just another peak? Would life be a dull, downhill slide from here? That seemed possible.

When my turn to go ashore came, the bos'n whistled, "Now hear this! Now hear this! The liberty party fall in on the hangar deck. The liberty party fall in on the hangar deck." The ship provided a bag lunch and a canteen of water. The boat rode through a comatose harbor. All activities, save those of the boats from our fleet, were at a standstill. Docks were wrecked or empty. A disabled battleship floated nearby at Yokasuka Navy Yard. Yokohama sprawled in dreary ruin. Small, thin, dull-eyed, exhausted people struggled to scratch out a life in the wreckage of their city. Some young men wearing combinations of mufti and military garb cast quick, angry glances at us. Others simply turned away. It's hard to imagine how I would have felt and acted had the situation been reversed. Yet it was even harder for me to dredge up feelings of sympathy or pity for them while images of my lost squadron mates remained fresh in my memory. I wandered about the streets of Yokohama for several hours, until one wrecked building began to look like all the others. At some places, the strong odor of decaying flesh was sickening. I imagined that it came from bodies buried beneath great, dusty mounds of fallen masonry. I found nothing entertaining there, only another sad lesson in the waste of war. One day ashore was enough for me.

The next day, our airplanes were moved to the flight deck and hundreds of cots were set up on the hangar deck. A hoard of enlisted army men milled about and settled down for the voyage to Hawaii. After being absent from my sleeping compartment for a few hours, I returned and stumbled against something as I switched on the light. It was a cot occupying most of the open deck space. An Army lieutenant snoozed on it, his gear stowed beneath. He roused, sat up, and said, "I'm Joe." Perhaps Bill Mauldin's original GI Joe had been promoted. He would bunk with us at least as far as Hawaii.

The following morning the bos'n's whistle shrilled through the ship, "Now hear this! Now hear this! The anchor detail lay forward to weigh anchor. The anchor detail lay forward to weigh anchor."

After fourteen days at anchor, the *Ticonderoga* sounded her deep-throated horn, glided out of the anchorage, and stood out to sea again. Japan faded astern.

Hawaii was eight days away, which meant another eight days of monotonous shipboard routine without work obligations for us, not much different from lying at anchor. Vic and I continued our routine of playing bridge all night and sleeping all day. Not even the constant chipping and painting of the deck nor the bos'n's whistle and his order, "Now hear this! Now hear this! Sweepers, man your brooms, clean sweep-down fore and aft. Sweepers, man your brooms, clean sweep-down fore and aft" could keep me awake.

I knew where in space I was headed, but not where my life was headed. I treaded water indecisively in a shifting tide of uncertainty. The ship knew where she was going, southeast toward Hawaii at fifteen knots.

A day out of Pearl Harbor, we were ordered to fly our aircraft ashore to Barbers Point Naval Air Station, adjacent to Pearl Harbor. The planes on the forward deck were catapulted to clear the deck for those near the stern, which were to be deck launched. A short, one-hour flight in the Hellcat put me back in the U.S.A. We stayed at Barbers Point while the *Ticonderoga* took aboard more passengers in Pearl Harbor and made a round-trip to California. In three weeks we would reboard her, bound for the Seattle-Tacoma area to celebrate Navy Day. Meanwhile, we vacationed in Hawaii.

Although unlike home, it beat being confined to an all-male society in a ship, as we had been for five months. We all suffered from alcohol and female deprivation. The first we satisfied at the Officers' Club. The second suffered from short supply in the Hawaiian Islands. Tsunamis of soldiers, marines, and sailors had washed over them, coming and going to the war. The local women were bored by the sight of us. We all knew the search was fruitless, except Vic. He visited his nurse friend on Maui while we slaked our thirst at the club.

After a few days, Sam and I decided to break the Oahu beach, bar, and bed cycle by flying to another island. I scrounged a Hellcat and he a dive-bomber from our squadrons, and we headed to Barking Sands Naval Air Station on Kauai, the next island, a hundred miles northwest of Oahu. Sam had his aircrewman with him. We made a flying sight-seeing tour of the island and then a steep approach to the air station. We planned to stay the night in town, so we had our liberty uniforms with us. That is, we had them until the sharp descent. Sam's aircrewman had his going-ashore uniform in a handbag on his lap. He opened the cockpit canopy as we started down. The handbag drifted upward out of reach and was last seen tumbling toward the ocean. He fretted that he could not leave the air station dressed in his flying gear, but we explained the circumstances to the security personnel and he was permitted to stay with us.

Kauai was among the dullest places I had ever visited. The towns were small, hotel rooms scarce and Spartan, food bad, booze expensive, and the population withdrawn. When the sun set, all life stopped. Only the beaches and tropical mountainous scenery made the visit worth the effort. Under different circumstances it could have been a delight, but I continued to have uncertain, treading-water sensations. The war's end had deprived me of a goal that had sustained me for years. The pull of home and the uncertainty of the future made the present trivial. The next afternoon, we were back at Barbers Point in time to open the club bar.

The future loomed on other minds as well. Late in the evening, a drunken aviator stumbled into the bar, uniform in disarray, hatless, and bleeding from a cut in his scalp. It was Vic. His disjointed story explained that his nurse friend had demanded, amid tears and hand wringing, some commitment from him to make their relationship permanent, something he wouldn't do. She had then told him their affair was at an end and asked him to leave. After flying back from Maui, he took a shortcut to the club along a wooded walkway, past some enlisted men's barracks. There, one or more men attacked and beat him. He didn't know the attackers or why the assault had taken place. He seemed strangely bewildered by the attack and melancholy that his romance had ended so abruptly.

When the *Ticonderoga* returned, we were ready to leave. We had seen enough of Hawaii for the present. Ahead lay a ten-day voyage to Seattle. We quickly slipped back into our bridge all night and sleep all day routine. In three days, we were out of the trade winds and into the prevailing westerlies, and then the "roaring forties." The forties were roaring, the wind on our stern. When you stood on the flight deck facing forward, the ship cruising at fifteen knots, the wind on your back topped thirty-five knots, a steady wind over the water of at least fifty knots. With the enormous fetch in the North Pacific, waves had built to an average height of twenty-five feet. As one old-timer put it, "there's nothing between Siberia and us except a barbed wire fence, and it's down."

We knew the ship was suffering because she cried plaintively night and day with each pitch and roll. I remembered those sounds of metal structures bending and working against each other during the typhoon off Japan. Those rotten sea conditions continued until we rounded Cape Flattery into the Strait of Juan de Fuca, where our first view of North America was the snow-covered mountains on the Olympic Peninsula to starboard and green Vancouver Island to port. Home lay just ahead.

In calm water inside the strait, the ship launched us and we flew ashore to Sand Point Naval Air Station near Seattle. The ship docked at Tacoma, where she would remain until after Navy Day. At Sand Point, hundreds of aviators home from the war were in a boozing frenzy at the club. We joined them. Several smoky connected rooms were crowded with reveling aviators. Occasionally, the PA system would page an officer for a telephone call.

One page was for Lt. Zar Begovich. It was such an unusual name that I knew he must have been the man I'd known in high school at Helena. The first time his name was called, I could not locate him.

I heard his name called again. This time, a Marine officer responded and headed for the telephone. I intercepted him when he finished his call and identified myself. He acknowledged that he remembered me, but I was surprised and chagrined when he indicated that he was more interested in returning to drink with his buddies than talking to me even briefly. Welcome home! His behavior was so unlike any other I had experienced with my former schoolmates that it stunned me. Anger welled up. "Screw him," I thought as he turned his back and walked away. I never saw him again.

Decision time rested on everyone's mind. If you had sufficient "points," you could be discharged or request an additional assignment. Without sufficient points, you would be reassigned. Most of the men had decided long ago. Sam wanted out, but Vic had decided to stay in, at least temporarily. I had sufficient points but fence-sat.

The end of October neared. If I got out then, school seemed the only reasonable course for me, since I lacked salable professional skills yet, unless flying could be considered one. If I were to return to school, I would have to wait until the end of January to begin the spring semester. After the excitement of flying in the Navy, the high living, camaraderie, and the prestige of officer status that went with it, school as I remembered it would have been dull. Perhaps I would like the peacetime Navy. I would never know if I didn't try it. By now, I felt ambivalent and vaguely fatalistic about flying. It did not have much intellectual stimulation for me, and the danger involved always lurked in the back of my mind. The pending GI bill made college more attractive and financially less painful. I finally chose a middle course. I would hang on to the Navy tit for a few months by accepting another assignment that would test my taste for the peacetime Navy. If I didn't like it, I would quit and return to school. The decision thus made, I waited for orders at Seattle and lived it up as before.

My orders were thirty days leave, then report to Naval Air Station, Atlanta, Georgia, where I would enter the Instrument Flight Instructors School (IFIS) pronounced "if iss." That sounded like an appropriate destination for someone as "iffy" as I. The squadron held a disbanding party at a restaurant called the Twin Teepees, with too much booze, food, and expense, and too few women, that produced another hangover and regrets. How many times had I been drunk? That question scared me. The squadron melted away until only the administrative officer and the skipper remained.

Our squadron book described our skipper, Lt. Cdr. Walter A. Haas: With good humor, firmness, and a remarkable knowledge of aerial combat tactics gleaned from experience, this new skipper carried on with the greatest success after the loss of our first commander. Spurred by an ever-increasing love for flying, "Walt" first tried his wings as a civilian glider pilot, then found himself flying fighters for the navy many months before Pearl Harbor. He got around—the Coral Sea and Midway, for instance. He clipped six Japanese planes from the sky and received two Navy Crosses from a grateful nation. Then he took fledgling pilots under his wing at Miami and Jacksonville to teach them the trade. The ability to make friends, an exemplary moral code, and wealth of good cheer were uniquely combined in him. A pilot of unsurpassed skill, Walt had our unqualified confidence at his command.

For me, the most remarkable aspect of this tribute is that I knew nothing of his aviating exploits until the squadron book was published. In fact, only a few senior officers must have known them because none of the junior officers with whom I associated ever spoke of his combat experience nor did he ever speak of it in squadron meetings. His modesty was admirable.

I shook the skipper's hand. I would not do that again until forty-three years later when we would meet at a squadron reunion. I headed for northern Idaho to visit Dad.

20

On Leave after the War

Dad now made a comfortable living as manager of a small milling operation in Wallace. His years of promoting and managing similar shoestring operations had finally paid off. He enjoyed greater financial security than anyone else in the family. Having established himself among the mining industry people in the area, he had become a member of social organizations and kept regular company with an old-maid schoolteacher, Ella, who was about his age. He had abandoned hope of reconciliation with Mother.

Wallace, a blue-collar mining town, contained many more men than women. In uniform with a couple of rows of campaign ribbons below my wings, I was an oddity and a source of curiosity to the natives. Dad tried valiantly to keep me occupied and entertained. He introduced me to his friends, and we made a couple of excursions to nearby lakes hunting for ducks, with no success. Entertainment sources were scarce: the Elks Club of which Dad was a member, a movie theater, bowling alley, and many bars, pretty slim pickings for someone fresh from Hawaii, Seattle, and the excitement and camaraderie of a fighter squadron. In the evening,

I snooped around a few bars. The women there were friendly but tough looking; possessive men lurked nearby, not friendly to strangers who talked to women they thought were theirs.

Dad's friend Ella I ranked as a cipher. Her main interests were buying and wearing hats and commenting on the performance of waitresses in restaurants. She played a lousy game of bridge and didn't know it. Her affection for Dad redeemed her flaws. He must have craved companionship though he had never spoken of it, but seemingly remained self-contained and immune to negative effects of family and business disappointments that discourage most people. He told me he had an interest in a mining prospect in the mountains of west-central Idaho and hoped I would help him check it out the following spring. It sounded intriguing, but I would have to let him know later.

The deadening atmosphere in Wallace hastened my departure after a week. I moved on to visit Helena and Butte before heading for California. In Helena, my high school classmates had been trickling home from the war for several weeks. They were easy to find in the local watering places, where we swapped war stories and pretended to be modest about our warrior achievements. I called Malcolm Streeter, who had been my shipmate on the *Ticonderoga*. We went to the high school and wandered about the halls and classrooms hoping to see the faculty. We found a few. The old principal, Mr. Wahl, the first person I had met in Helena, was one. The strain of being the principal had become too much for him, so he had quit and begun teaching mathematics. We visited him after a class. He seemed pleased to see us and freely admitted that even teaching was more strain than he could take. To illustrate, he held up his arms. The pits showed great circles of perspiration on his shirt. It was painful to see how that kind man was suffering. What could we say?

Helen, a fondly remembered schoolmate, still lived there. I visited her and her firstborn in a small apartment. Her husband, Bob Clark, also a classmate and then a Marine aviator, had not yet returned from the war. When I arrived, Helen was scrubbing diapers in the kitchen sink. She continued as we exchanged news and reminiscences. The doorbell rang. Another naval aviator in uniform, a friend of her husband's, made a social call. Helen continued scrubbing and rinsing diapers through a long three-sided conversation. That was my first peek at the messy underside of marital bliss. Eventually, the other aviator and I left and spent the evening visiting the nightspots of Helena. I would see him again in Atlanta.

At the School of Mines in Butte, the faculty had not changed much. Students were scarce. The flood of returning veterans had not yet arrived. I saw Mac, my old coach, and Joey, my schoolmate who had crashed in a torpedo bomber near Norfolk. He was enrolled as a graduate student in geology. I found Joey in a laboratory, looking down a petrographic microscope, scarred, lame, gloomy, and unresponsive, a shadow of his former robust, cheerful self. His war wounds were multiple and deep. On top of his crippled body had been piled the failure of his marriage. I couldn't draw him into a conversation, and he didn't encourage me to extend my visit, so I left, never to see him again.

I wandered about the campus and strolled through Butte's city center. Nothing much had changed. It remained even drearier than I had remembered. Butte vaguely repelled me and stirred feelings of unease about returning to the School of Mines if I didn't continue in the Navy. It might be different later when my schoolmates had returned from the service. I experienced the disquieting feeling reported by others that "you can't go back; things will be smaller and not as you remember them." After a day and a night, I left for San Francisco with a feeling of relief.

San Francisco was now more to my taste. Its vitality, variety, and charming setting attracted me. I enjoyed the anonymity of the city and yet being close to Mother and my sisters. I slept in one of their apartments, took most of my meals with them, and borrowed their cars for visits to nightspots. The favorite hangout for

naval aviators and women interested in them remained the
Yankee Doodle Bar on Powell Street. I often wondered how it had
become so popular. A hundred other bars not far away, with the
same booze and essentially the same atmosphere, attracted a fraction of the business. From late afternoon until after midnight the
place crawled with naval officers. It had a long bar along one side
and one row of tables along the other. Between them milled a
crowd of officers talking, lapping up booze, and maneuvering for
positions near the women who occupied most of the bar stools.
In that highly competitive climate, I performed poorly, but it was
a stimulating atmosphere in which I occasionally met aviators I
had known in the air group or somewhere in the training program. I clung to the past.

Pathetically, we were trying to keep hold of that roller-coaster
aviation life: kind and cruel, soft and hard, uplifting and degrad-
ing, beautiful and ugly, sweet and bitter, soothing and frightening,
safe and dangerous, playful and grinding, loving and hateful, exhilarating and boring, a life that inexorably seeped away from us, a
part of our lives the like of which we feared we would never see
again. We clung to it tenaciously, but knew it must slip from our
grasp. We secretly dreaded the uncertainty of the life that would
take its place. We had floated on a river of surprises that now carried us toward a placid, unfamiliar sea of peace and certainty, and
we fruitlessly fought the current.

Before me now beckoned a taste of the peacetime naval life at the
air station in Atlanta. I approached that experience with a wait-and-
see attitude not conducive to fetching forth maximum effort.

21

Leaving the Peacetime Navy

I can't remember the Atlanta Air Station being significantly different from any of the many others I had known. They all had an institutional aspect, but of course, that's what they were. The administration building was marked by a flagpole in front; enlisted barracks were neatly aligned; aircraft hangars faced a tarmac on which aircraft were parked in precise rows like stuffed birds in a museum; gray Navy vehicles parked or moved about the streets; buildings had large numbers on them and discreet signs with acronyms, suggesting the activities that took place inside. In short, a familiar place I had come to know and understand, more like home than any other setting I knew. It gave me a feeling of security and comfort to be back under the protection of the naval organization, with its clear-cut lines of command and status. If I could function well within the military system, there seemed a reasonably satisfying career ahead of me. I knew the system, but I had reservations about my ability to fit into it for a long career. I had never been keen on running long distances.

This air station trained aviators to become instrument flight instructors. Graduates would, in turn, instruct cadets in the training command or give refresher training to pilots at other stations. Most of the in-flight training employed an aircraft I had never heard of until then, the NH1, a high-wing monoplane, single-engine, three-passenger aircraft. On a typical training flight, a pilot and copilot flew in front seats, with a pilot under instruction in a windowless compartment in the rear.

A training flight was pure drudgery, long hours of flying radio ranges and executing precision climbing, turning, and descending patterns. These maneuvers required a high level of concentration that had completion as their only reward, with no joy in the antic-ipation of repeating them. They confirmed my belief that some-one had invented this activity to take the pleasure out of flying and to simultaneously separate the dedicated flight-lover from the rest of us. Ground school and "flights" in the earthbound Link trainers rounded out the official training activities.

Atlanta was a great liberty town. The situation at one local nightclub, crowded with women out for a good time, reminded me of an often-repeated anecdote, probably apocryphal, about an aviator who was observed going from table to table and saying something to the women. The women would laugh or look shocked. Commonly, after he had spoken to several women, one would laugh, finish her drink, and leave with him. When asked what he had said to them, he said, "I just asked, do you fuck? It saves a lot of time and money."

I became involved in a casual party that turned into a nasty fight between a man and a woman in which blood was shed. I left on foot before the shore patrol arrived. As I walked alone down a dark street, shame and regret plagued me. How had I gotten into that sordid situation? My senses of decency and right were eroding.

Winter in Georgia meant rain. Some pilots cursed the bad weather, but others, like me, secretly saw it as an approaching hol-iday. I worked out with the air station basketball team and made the traveling squad but never played enough to feel comfortable with the team. Early on, I became acquainted with an enlisted

WAVE named Eleanor, a tall, blond, willowy woman with genteel southern manners and a drawl to match. We spent much time together in Atlanta and would occasionally hike about the countryside surrounding the base. This went on for several weeks. We liked each other, but something was missing that baffled me and kept us at the hand-holding, good-night-kiss stage.

One evening at the Officers' Club, an Army officer on crutches clumped his way across the dance floor and stopped at my table. It turned out to be Don Servin, with whom I had played basketball at Helena High School. I had not seen him for six years. The Japanese had shot off one of his legs. Don had a car and an apartment, and Eleanor and I spent some time with him and his wife on quiet outings in the country. I felt that my friendship with Eleanor would develop into something more intimate, but it was not to be.

In early February, as I neared the end of the training program at Atlanta, my old buddy Vic arrived unexpectedly at the air station. He was ferrying an aircraft from somewhere to somewhere else. Bad weather kept him with us for two days. That was time enough for a reunion and partying with Eleanor and my other newly acquired friends. Following his visit, I sensed that Eleanor was somewhat cool to me and less available. Thinking back on Vic's visit, I recalled that they had spent much time near each other exchanging y'alls and drinking. Apparently, his vaunted charm had been at work.

During my stay in Atlanta, I again felt that without the war, flying had lost its purpose and urgency for me. Again I treaded water, drifting with no clear destination. I finally decided that the peacetime Navy and I were not meant for each other. In the spring I would join up with Dad in his mining venture in Idaho and then go back to school. My request for release from active duty was approved, with orders to the Separation Center in San Francisco. There were no tearful good-byes from Eleanor, just empty promises to keep in touch.

Checking with Flight Operations, I learned that a twin-engine DC-3 was leaving for the San Francisco Bay Area at noon. I gathered up my gear and lugged it to Operations, where a lieutenant was filing a flight plan. I added my name to the plan and climbed aboard, joining several other passengers, and settled into a bucket seat for a long ride. After takeoff, I stood in the cockpit looking over the pilots' shoulders, watching them pore over aeronautical charts on which they followed highways and railroads toward the Gulf Coast. We flew on visual flight rules at low altitude toward an overnight stop at New Orleans. I returned to my seat and stared disinterestedly at the endless piney woods, towns, and rivers sliding under us, as I thought and rethought my decision to leave the Navy. Waves of uncertainty and regret washed over me, but what I had done could not be undone. Soon the Gulf sparkled up ahead, and we changed course along the coast into NAS New Orleans, on the shore of Lake Pontchartrain.

I declined an invitation from a couple of pilots to go into town for the evening. Drinking and carousing did not fit my mood that night. I remembered the night, years earlier, when Paul and I, fresh out of cadet training and bound for Florida, had received a lesson there about the wiles of women and learned of the limited charm of our golden wings. It struck me that then I had been happily going east toward training in combat-type aircraft, not knowing that the dying would begin. Now, I headed west sadly, toward the end of flying, which had lost its meaning, to begin the rest of my life.

The next morning, we took off early, and hugged the Gulf Coast as far as Houston before slanting inland. Off to port somewhere in the humid haze sat Corpus Christi, the factory that had made me an aviator, full of baseless pride and vacant dreams of glory. We refueled at San Antonio where, in a railroad yard, fifty other cadets and I had joyously sluiced away the grime of five bathless days on a troop train by stripping to the skin in a cloudburst. It seemed that a film of my life of becoming an aviator was running in reverse. The rest of the day and the next, that film continued to rewind as we droned along that railroad, a casual scrawl on the monotonous plains of west Texas, to El Paso and the desert

Southwest to San Bernardino. There we turned north up the Central Valley, still on the railroad, past Livermore, where I had flown the Yellow Perils, then to the shining bay.

We landed at Alameda, where, signaled to a parking slot, the pilot shut down the engines for the last time, an eerie silence after a storm. Chocks thudded under the wheels like exclamation points ending a chapter of my life. The earth felt good. I waved goodbye to my flying companions, just other men who had faintly brushed my life, picked up my bags, leaned head down into a cold breeze off the bay, and strode into what I hoped would be a more meaningful life.

Having abandoned the idea of making a career as an aerial warrior, I joined Dad in his mining prospect in the mountains of Idaho. That too seemed to be taking me nowhere, nor did returning to the School of Mines in Butte suit my changed perspective. California drew me back, and I entered the University of California, Berkeley, as an undergraduate student in geology. That led me ultimately to a master's degree, employment with the California Division of Mines in San Francisco, marriage, and a leave of absence to spend a year with my bride in France. Back in the States as the Korean War was winding down, the Navy recalled me for six months as a photo intelligence officer in Washington, D.C. A civilian again, I was hired by Texaco to look for oil in the Ventura Basin of coastal California.

To my good fortune, Texaco assigned me to its offshore exploratory program, in which I supervised a group of pioneering geological scuba divers collecting geological data from the seafloor along the Santa Barbara Channel coast. That group turned out to be renowned academic marine geologists. In 1956 they taught me to dive in calm water in the kelp beds west of Santa Barbara. Working with these geologists stimulated me to quit Texaco in 1962 at age thirty-nine, with a wife and three kids. I bought out one of the consulting diving geologists and entered the doctoral program in marine geology at the University of

Southern California in Los Angeles. Working as a diving geologist to support my family during that four-year program, I was awarded a Ph.D. in 1965.

Then, while I was president of our consulting firm, we began enlarging the company's capabilities by acquiring research vessels and seismic systems, and building two-man submarines to carry our seafloor geological exploration to a water depth of one thousand feet. It was a classic "boot-strapping operation" needing no outside financing. In all I made more than 1,000 scuba dives and 250 dives in submarines as pilot and observer. Diving and piloting a submarine turned out to be as dramatic and engaging as flying. The remainder of my working life was spent gathering and supervising the collection of hard-to-get geological and geophysical data from the seafloor for oil exploration, engineering projects, and biological studies in such diverse places as California, Canada, Alaska, Mexico, the East Coast, Eniwetok Atoll, South and Central America, New England, Gibraltar, and the Mediterranean Sea.

I now live on a coastal hill in southern California where my gaze often falls on the ocean and the distant Channel Islands, stirring memories of my life in the sky and sea.

Index

accidents: dive-bombing, 71; in Hawaii, 137; in Hellcats, 102–4, 131–32; on *Randolph*, 114; in SBDs, 67–69

aerobatics, 38–40

aircraft carriers, landing on, 71–72, 77–82, 116–17, 132–35

aircrewmen, 72

Air Group 81, 135–36

Air Group 87, 1, 96–99, 101–2, 108–9, 121–22

Air Group 94, 138

Alameda, Calif., Naval Air Station, 120–23, 125–26, 201

Alaska, 144

Alturas, Calif., Civilian Pilot Training at, 12–15

antiblackout suits, 107

Aomori Bay, 177

Apra, Guam, 154–55

Atlanta, Georgia, Naval Air Station, 191, 197–99

Atlantic City, N.J., 96–99

atomic bombs, 176–77

Baker, Capt. Felix, 118

Barbers Point Naval Air Station, 188, 189

Barking Sands Naval Air Station, 189

barrier patrols, 146–47

Bataan, 154

Bateman (pilot), 142, 164

beam, on the, 49

Bill (lieutenant in strikes on Honshū), 177

blackouts, 70–71, 105–7

blinker reading, 22–23

Bogan, Rear Admiral, 154, 171–72

bogies, 170, 179

bomb fuses, proximity, 176–77

Bombing-Fighting 87 squadron, 121–22. *See also* VBF-87

bombs, 69–70, 151, 176–77

Bougainville, 94–95

Brisette (Porter's aircrewman), 171

B-29s, 154–55

Butcher (replacement pilot), 172–75

Butte, Mont., 195

Cabo San Lucas, 120

California Division of Mines, San Francisco, 202

Cassidy, Al, 135–36, 178

catapult launch, 113–14

cease-fire declaration, 179–80,
183–84
Cecil Field, 64–72
check flights, 34–38
Chicago, 80
Civilian Pilot Training (CPT): at
Alturas, 12–15; at Susanville,
4–11
Clark, Bob, 194–95
Clark, Helen, 194–95
combat air patrols (CAPs), 119,
141–42, 172–75
Combat Intelligence Center (CIC),
146
commissioning as naval aviator,
62–63
Copahee, 126–29
Corpus Christi, Tex., 44–51. *See also*
Main Side
Corsair fighters, 181–83
Crawford, Lieutenant, 67–68
Cross, Russell, 126
Cuddihy Field, 47–51

Daitō Islands, 151
dating, 40–41
Del Monte, Calif., 15
Del Monte Resort Hotel, 16–17,
25–28. *See also* preflight school
demobilization plan, 184
Dick: car trip to Mexico, 55–57; at
Cecil Field, 64, 66; death, 115; at
Kingsville, 52–53; at Main Side,
62; organization of, 59–60; on
Randolph, 112; at Wildwood, 85,
88, 93
discipline at Glenview, 79–81

dive-bombers, 64, 67–72, 104–6,
131–32
Dobson (check flight pilot), 37–38
Douglas Aircraft Company, 68

Elder, Donald, 132–35
Essex, 154

Fargo, N.Dak., 2–3, 83
"fighter sweep," 150
flight instructors: at Alturas (Bill),
13, 14–15; at Livermore, 33; at
Susanville (Marty), 7–9
flight training. *See* Atlanta,
Georgia, Naval Air Station;
Cecil Field; Livermore Naval
Air Station
Florida, 64–65, 73–76
flying: attitude toward, 33–35, 196;
on instruments, 48–49; night,
42–43, 60–61, 132–35
Ford Island, 139, 140–41
Foss, Joe, 40

gasoline, low-octane, 67–69
Ginger Base, 179
Glenview, Ill., Naval Air Station,
75–82
graveyard spiral, 107
grayouts, 70–71
Great Lakes Naval Training
Center, 7, 43
"Group Grope to End All Group
Gropes," 183
Grumman, 231–32. *See also* Hellcat,
Grumman F6F
Guam, 154–55

Guam, 144
gunnery runs, 55

Haas, Lt. Cdr. Walter A., 125, 130, 166, 192
Halsey, Admiral, 144, 183
Hawaii, 129–38, 187–90
Helena, Mont., 194–95
Hellcat, Grumman F6F: accidents, 102–4, 131–32; dive-bombing training in, 131–32; first flight in, 97–98; fuel capacity, 148, 151
Hiroshima, 176, 184
Hiroshima Castle, 171
Hokkaido, 176
Honshū, 176–77
Hunters Point Naval Shipyard, 120–21
Hyuga, 166–67

Idaho, 76, 82–84, 193–94, 199, 202
Independence, 144
Inland Sea, 169–71
Instrument Flight Instructors School (IFIS), 191–92
Irō-Zaki, 178
Iwakuni Air Base, 161

Jacksonville, Fla., 73–75
jeep carrier ("Kaiser Coffin"), 126–29

Kagoshima Bay, 148
Kahului, Naval Air Station, 129, 138
kamikazes: attacks on *Ticonderoga,* 139, 140; description in

"September Song II," 173; destruction of, 145–48, 157–60; and reorganization of Air Group 87, 122; strategy, 156
Kauai, 189
Kingsville, 51–61
Kōbe-Nagoya area, 175
Koontz, Art, 131–32, 138
Korean War, 202
Kure Naval Air Station, 161, 167–68
Kyūshū, 148–51

Lake Michigan, 77–82
landings, 34–36; field carrier practice, 71–72, 132–35; night, 43, 132–35; qualification, 77–82; timing of, 116–17
Lassen Junior College, 4–6
Lerch, Ensign, 146–47
Leyte, 151–54
liberties, 41–42, 198
lighthouse at Irō-Zaki, strafing of, 178
link trainers, 49–50
Livermore Naval Air Station: assignment to, 25, 29–44; barracks life at, 30–31; curriculum, 33–40; flight instructors at, 33
Lou Booth's Club, 92–93

Macarata, 152–53
MacArthur, Douglas, 94, 95
Main Side, 46–47, 62–63
Maloelap Atoll, 141–42
Manteo, N.C., 104–5
Mantis, Jim, 172–75
Martin, Cadet, 23

Matsuyama West Airfield, 160

Maui, 129–38

Maxwell, Cdr. Porter W., 89, 125, 130, 157–66

McAllen, Tex., 56–57

Mexico, 55–57

Miller, Bill, 158–59, 163, 164, 179, 181–83

Minami Daitō Jima, 151

Misawa Airfield, 177

Missouri, 144

Mogmog, 144

Molokai, 138

Montana School of Mines, 2, 6, 195

Monterrey, 154, 173

Montgomery, G. C., 79

Morse code, 22–23

Nansei Shoto (Ryukyu Islands), 145

napalm bombs, 151

Navy: entry into, 3–6; peacetime, 191–92, 197–99

New Orleans, 64–65, 200

New Orleans, Naval Air Station, 200

NHIs, 198

night field carrier landing practice, 132–35

Niihama Airfield, 162

Norfolk, Va., 84–85

North Island Naval Air Station, 126

Oceana, Va., Naval Air Station: dive-bomb practice at, 104–6; organization of, 100–101; recreation at, 107–8; tragedies while at, 102–4; transfer to, 99–100

O'Connell, Joe, 137

Okinawa, 1, 145–48

Ominato Naval Base, 177

outside loops, 39

outside slow roll, 39

Panama, 118–20

Paul (cadet from Los Angeles), 31; in accident, 71; assignment to dive-bombers, 64; and landing, 35; at Main Side, 62; on train to Florida, 64–65

Pearl Harbor, 139, 188

Piper Cubs, 7–15

Porter, Raymond, 171

Port of Spain, Trinidad, 117–18

Potsdam ultimatum, 177

preflight school, 15–28; academic program, 20–23; athletics program, 19–25; attitude toward, 30; choir, 22; graduation ceremony, 25–27; meals at, 21–22

proximity fuses, 176–77

Pud: on aerobatics, 38–39; assignment to Livermore, 25; to Great Lakes, 43; initial meeting, 17–19; on living conditions at Livermore, 29–30; on preflight school curriculum, 20–22, 24, 27, 28; reunion with in San Francisco, 124–25

Pusan, Korea, 169–70

Rabaul, 94

radar, 63

Radford, Rear Admiral, 144

radio range flying, 49

Randolph: accidents on, 114; daily routine on, 119; description of, 101–2, 110–12; rendezvous with Air Group 87, 108–9; shakedown cruise, 112–20; in Task Group 38.3, 154

refueling, 169

Reynosa, Mexico, 56–57

"Rocks and Shoals," 21, 128

Ronchi Airfield, 148–51

"routine training flights," 104

Sable, 77–78, 80, 81–82

Sam: in Air Group 87, 122; bond with, 72–73; at Cecil Field, 66; discharge, 191; on experiences with women, 95–96; at Glenview, 77–78; in Hawaii, 189; on *Hyuga,* 166–67; on leave in San Francisco, 123; on liberty at Port of Spain, 118; at Norfolk, 84–85; in Oceana, 99–100, 108; on *Randolph,* 112; in SBDs, 68–69; separation from, 97; on *Ticonderoga,* 139; trip to Tinian, 154–55; at Wildwood, 88

Samar, 152–53

Sand Point Naval Air Station, 190

San Francisco, 3–5; liberty in, 41–42; return to aboard *Randolph,* 120–25; return to after leaving Navy, 199–201; return to after war, 195–96; work with California Division of Mines in, 202

San Francisco State College, 123–24

Saratoga, 93

SB2C Helldivers ("the Beast,") 88, 91, 94, 95, 115

SBDs, 67–69, 81–82

Schultz, Ensign, 17, 20, 28, 78–80

Seattle, 191

Secrest, Hank, 24–25, 126

"September Song II," 172–75

Servin, Don, 199

Shangri-La, 144

Shipley Bay, 135–36

skip bombing, 95

smuggling, 56–57

SNJs, 52–55, 60–61

solo flight, first, 9

Stearman N2Ss ("Yellow Peril"), 32–33

strafing of airfields, 149–51, 156–65, 168

Streeter, Malcolm, 140, 194

submarine air combat patrol, 178

submarines, piloting, 203

Susanville, Calif., 4–11

Tacoma, 190

Taroa Island, 141–42

Task Group 38.3, 154–56

Task Group 38.4, 144–45

Texaco, 202–3

Third Fleet, U.S., 180

Ticonderoga, 1; combat air patrols over, 141–42; departure from Ford Island, 140–41; description of, 139–40; orders to, 138; at Pearl Harbor, 188; recreation on, 152–53; repairs in Guam, 154–55; in Task Group 38.3, 154–56; in Task Group 38.4, 144–51; in Tokyo Bay, 184–88

Tinian, 154–55

Tokyo, 178–79, 186

Tokyo Bay, 184–88
Tone, 171
Trinidad, 117–18
typhoon season, 171–72

Ulithi, 141–43
uniforms, 62
University of California, Berkeley, 202
University of Southern California, Los Angeles, 203
unusual attitude training, 50–51

Vaughn, Eppa, 167
VB-87 (dive-bomber squadron), 85
VBF-87 (bombing-fighting squadron), 130–31, 145
Vernalis, Naval Air Station, 125
Vernon family: Dad, 5–6, 26, 76, 82–84, 124, 193–94, 199, 202; Janice (sister), 26; Mother, 3–5, 26–27, 73–76, 82–84, 123–24, 195–96; Myrl (sister), 26; Rosemary (sister), 26, 73–76, 82–84
VF-87 squadron, 97–99, 145
Vic: in Atlanta, 199; bond with, 72–73; as bridge partner, 119, 153, 188; at Cecil Field, 66; decision to remain in Navy, 191; on flight across Inland Sea, 170; on flying SBDs, 67–68; at Glenview, 77, 78–82; in Hawaii,

188, 189–90; on Maui, 129; on near collision with Corsairs, 183; at Norfolk, 84–85; in Oceana, 99–100, 107–8; at Port of Spain, 118; on proximity fuses, 177; on *Randolph,* 112; in San Francisco, 123; separation from, 97; on *Ticonderoga,* 139; transfer to Bombing-Fighting 87, 122; at Wildwood, 85–88
Vultee SNV ("Vultee Vibrator"), 48–49

Wahl, Mr., 194
Wallace, Idaho, 83–84, 193–94
Watsonville, Naval Air Station, 125
WAVEs, 50
Wildwood, N.J., Naval Air Station: assignment to, 85–87; description of, 88–89; recreation at, 92–96; squadron bonds formed at, 89–91
Wisconsin, 144
Wolverine, 77–78, 80
Woods, Fred, 168

Yankee Doodle Bar, 124, 196
"Yellow Peril" (Stearman N2S), 32–33
Yokohama, 186–87
Yontan, 145
Yontan Airfield, 147–48
Yorktown, 144

About the Author

James W. Vernon, a northern Minnesota native, spent parts of his boyhood in California, Nevada, and Montana. In 1942, after two years at the Montana School of Mines, Vernon began his naval aviation training. While serving aboard the carriers USS *Randolph* and *Ticonderoga* during the Second World War, he flew Hellcats with three Air Group 87 squadrons. Before the war's end, Vernon saw combat at Okinawa and Japan.

After World War II, Vernon earned a Ph.D. in geology, served in Korea as a photographic intelligence officer, and retired from the Naval Reserve as a lieutenant commander. As president of a geological scuba diving consulting company, he pioneered the application of manned submersibles to commercial geological exploration. During his career as an exploration geologist, Vernon traveled all over the world gathering geological and geophysical data from the seafloor.

Vernon now lives in California with his family on a hill overlooking the Santa Barbara Channel.

The Naval Institute Press is the book-publishing arm of the U.S. Naval Institute, a private, nonprofit, membership society for sea service professionals and others who share an interest in naval and maritime affairs. Established in 1873 at the U.S. Naval Academy in Annapolis, Maryland, where its offices remain today, the Naval Institute has members worldwide.

Members of the Naval Institute support the education programs of the society and receive the influential monthly magazine *Proceedings* and discounts on fine nautical prints and on ship and aircraft photos. They also have access to the transcripts of the Institute's Oral History Program and get discounted admission to any of the Institute-sponsored seminars offered around the country.

The Naval Institute also publishes *Naval History* magazine. This colorful bimonthly is filled with entertaining and thought-provoking articles, first-person reminiscences, and dramatic art and photography. Members receive a discount on *Naval History* subscriptions.

The Naval Institute's book-publishing program, begun in 1898 with basic guides to naval practices, has broadened its scope to include books of more general interest. Now the Naval Institute Press publishes about one hundred titles each year, ranging from how-to books on boating and navigation to battle histories, biographies, ship and aircraft guides, and novels. Institute members receive significant discounts on the Press's more than eight hundred books in print.

Full-time students are eligible for special half-price membership rates. Life memberships are also available.

For a free catalog describing Naval Institute Press books currently available, and for further information about subscribing to *Naval History* magazine or about joining the U.S. Naval Institute, please write to:

Membership Department

U.S. Naval Institute

291 Wood Road

Annapolis, MD 21402-5034

Telephone: 800-233-8764

Fax: 410-269-7940

Web address: www.usni.org